Eaglehawk Girl

Published by Brolga Publishing Pty Ltd
ABN 46 063 962 443
PO Box 12544
A'Beckett St
Melbourne, VIC, 8006
Australia

email: markzocchi@brolgapublishing.com.au

National Library of Australia
Cataloguing-in-Publication data
        Liz Low, author.
        ISBN 9780648327721 (paperback)

A catalogue record for this
book is available from the
National Library of Australia

NATIONAL
LIBRARY
OF AUSTRALIA

Cover design by Alice Cannet
Typesetting by Elly Cridland

BE PUBLISHED

Publish through a successful publisher. National Distribution through Woodslane Pty Ltd
International Distribution to the United Kingdom, North America
Sales Representation to South East Asia
Email: markzocchi@brolgapublishing.com.au

Eaglehawk Girl

A free range child

Liz Low

Contents

Foreword

Independent mobility, or the freedom to move unsupervised, is an integral part of growing up. It provides children and young people opportunities to explore their cognitive, emotional, social, physical and spatial boundaries. Although scary at times, this type of freedom supports confidence through competence. Kids learn to negotiate the world around them from experiencing it first-hand.

My own research over the past decade shows that independent mobility has significantly decreased in the last sixty years. In richer countries, parental concern about traffic and fear of stranger danger mostly explain this trend. In less developed nations, children have to travel further distances, manage dangerous terrain and travel in groups or stay home after school to avoid exploitation. Yet, Australia is one of the safest places on earth for kids. The web of safety provided by neighbours, strangers and other kids remains strong. Its form and participants might have changed since Liz Low's childhood, but I believe it is there. In our desire to protect our kids, it is important that we don't prevent them from learning about themselves, their talents and capabilities.

Liz Low's memoir reminds us that the ordinary is extraordinary when you're young. Through the incidental observations of a child, it offers insight into the challenges and rewards of growing up in a small community and facing changing circumstances. It shows us how important it is for kids to feel and be part of their communities in their own right.

Eaglehawk Girl also provides a portal to life in country Australia in the 1950–60s, a time when kids discovered their world as explorers and adventurers. I could relate to Liz's determination to escape from the bounds of acceptable feminine pursuits of the time, her eagerness to play football with the boys, the freedom of her bicycle and the joys of encountering the world by tram.

Being familiar with Eaglehawk, I really enjoyed her rich descriptions of the town, now a suburb of Bendigo. It was obvious to me that Liz considers her environment as much a part of the family as the people in her life. It is as active as she is, in her play and relationships.

As Liz highlights, she was a free-range girl. Being free-range brought a variety of challenges, surprises and moments of accomplishment, which are only possible with a positive engagement with risk and a willingness to trust.

Dr Julie Rudner
Community Planning and Development
La Trobe University. Bendigo Campus

Preface

'Between stimulus and response there is a space. In that space is our power to choose our response. In our response lies our growth and our freedom.'

– Viktor E. Frankl

Chapter One
Watery World

I'm just five. It's a Saturday afternoon in early summer and the rain is still bucketing down. I'm sick of hearing it roar on our corrugated iron roof and I'm fed up with being inside. I go out the fly-wire door on to the front verandah and see that our gravel street is full of muddy puddles. Then I remember the gutters. They'll be full!

I run out the driveway gate and look. Yes, the gutter is full of rushing, turbulent water. It's like a little river racing past my feet, and it doesn't smell of drains because there's so much water. I've never seen anything like it. I only know water that lies still and flat in the lake or in the dribble of the Eaglehawk Creek at the bottom of a stone and brick channel. Mum has been reading *Wind in the Willows* to me and I love its watery world. I wonder if this is what it was like for Mole when he first saw the lively, vigorous water outside Ratty's front door.

I like our deep bluestone and red-brick gutters which carry away our bath and sink water. Usually, the gutter holds a bright green ribbon of slime with patches of grey sludge, and the trickle of water moves slowly down towards the deep hole under the footpath on the corner. Each house has a little pipe leading to the gutter, and you can see grey, soapy water spurt out when someone has pulled the plug after doing the dishes or the washing.

I walk beside the current down to the underground pit which a brick cross drain enters before going under the road and then through the chook yard of the house with the pepper trees. Today, water hurtles in all directions, and I hear the pit thundering with the roaring, brown, frothy storm water fed into it. I follow the gutter upstream, towards the church and the main road. Here, there is more of a slope and the water is running faster.

I decide to take off my sandals and wade up the stream. The water pushes against my legs, sometimes up past my knees, and the smooth bricks feel nice under my feet.

What if I kneel?

The water surges up my thighs and soaks my shorts. I brace against the current. It's a bit cold but not too bad.

What if I sit?

The current pushes against my back, and I lie back, still with both hands on the bricks. I let go a bit. *Whoosh!* The water pushes and floats me feet first down the little river. I keep my hands ready to grab the bottom or sides. I am a little boat, Scuffy the Tugboat, in my Golden Book, free at last and surging and bobbing towards the open sea. I stand and push upstream and then whoosh away again. This time on my front, down past the front fences, rushing past the little drain pipes coming from the houses. I stop for the driveway bridges. I wouldn't fit under them.

I know I'm doing something strange, and I see a couple of women standing on their verandahs, arms folded across their aprons, looking at me, but I don't care. I'm having so much fun being swept around in the water.

Eventually, I get a bit cold and run home barefoot, turn up the drive and stand dripping at the back door. I'm pleased that I've remembered my sandals.

'Mum!' I yell, knowing I'm a bit wet to come inside.

Mum, in her apron, stands at the step of the kitchen door.

'I've been swimming in the gutter!'

'Oh, Lizzie! Leave your clothes here and get into the bath.'

She told me later that she had received a phone call.

'Mrs Trembath, do you know that Elizabeth's swimming in the gutter?'

I grew up in Eaglehawk, a small inland Victorian township near Bendigo. Our natural environment was hard, dry and crackly. Gum trees offered sparse shade and continually shed strips of bark and crescents of dull brown leaves. The roads were gravel. In summer, dry heat penetrated everywhere. Mum would be careful to close the windows of the house in the morning just when she judged that it was hotter outside than inside. Then the same decision in reverse would be made in the early evening when the sun had gone down. Despite this, our brick house would gradually heat up until we were living in a sort of heat bank.

I longed for the soft refreshment of swimming in cool water. However, going swimming wasn't always straightforward, and one Saturday afternoon down at the baths, I had got really burnt by the deceptive, early summer sun. My shoulders and back were red and stinging, and my shirt hurt my back. I was four, and sunburn was new to me. At bedtime, Mum had the idea of bathing my back in cold black tea. This was strange and a bit exciting. She made a pot of strong tea and we waited for it to cool. Then I lay on my bed, face down, and she gently wiped the cool tea over me with soft cotton wool. I loved her looking after me like that, all by myself in the quiet. My little sister, Jane, and baby brother, Richard, were asleep. The window was open after being closed all day and let the cooler evening air flow over my tea-dampened back. It was refreshing for a little while, but I had a restless night between sheets that felt scratchy and hard.

The next day was really hot again and I was dying to go to the pool. However, it was Sunday, and first I had to go to Sunday School, prickling in a hot dress, and then wait and wait. I still needed Mum to take me to the pool as I was too little and not yet able to swim properly.

'We'll wait till it's shady. You're too burnt.'

That was true. When I looked over my shoulder, I could see big, bubbly, transparent blisters on my back. I'd never had blisters before and felt proud of them.

By mid-afternoon, we finally got down to the baths which were unfenced and beside the lake in the park. Mum had found a soft T-shirt for me to wear over my bathers and blisters, and once she had parked the car under the trees near the band rotunda, I ran ahead into the bliss of cool water. At that time of day, the bubby pool was mostly shaded by the big gum trees in the park. The banks sloped toward the water and had green grass for the mothers to sit on with the tiny children and babies. I knew Mum would find a place to put down the rug for Jane, Richard and her.

I whooshed and splashed near the edge for a while and then looked around for Mum. There she was, sitting in her pretty summer dress on the rug, in the shade, with the other mothers and babies. I yelled and waved at her and she waved back. Now that I knew where she was and she knew where I was, I could go and play.

At one side of the shallow end, the sandy bottom sloped right up to the concrete edge and wall, like a beach, and I could run down it to whatever depth I liked and then plunge forward into the water before jumping to my feet again. The shallowest water was about up to my thighs. Then it gradually deepened out towards the posts and chain separating the big pool from the bubby pool. The pool was packed with children jumping around, playing and shouting and making the water brown and choppy.

I went over to the other side to see if the water was coming into the pool from the hidden pipe. Yes, it was. It flowed fast. A curved, shining arc of water poured over the flat lip of the concrete 'cave' in front of the pipe and plunged through the surface in a turmoil of bubbles. The other kids and I jostled to get a turn at sitting under the heavy, moving water. The little waterfall had eroded a gravelly hollow in the sandy bottom, and it was fun to crouch there, feeling the gravel underfoot. The water sploshed heavily on my head and shoulders and swirled around my underwater body.

I was pushed out of the way. It was someone else's turn.

'Erk! She's got blood! Erk!'

Kids were dancing and shouting around me in horrified excitement. I got out from the waterfall and peered over my shoulder. My T-shirt had grown round red splotches. *What's this! Oh, it's my blisters. They've burst. They're bleeding,* I realised. This was embarrassing.

I went back to Mum. The other mothers watched as Mum slipped me out of my pink and dripping T-shirt and mopped me up. I wasn't allowed back in, and soon we had to pack up and go home. And I hadn't had a go on the slide either.

The blisters healed up, and that was the end of burning for another summer. Over the years, I learnt that there always seemed to be the first burn of summer, and then you were sort of immunised for the rest of the season. At least, that's what we thought at the time. How wrong we were! Sunscreen didn't appear until I was about eighteen, but by then my skin had been badly damaged.

Mum must have found my early swimming attempts a bit nerve-racking to watch. They were a splashy, thrashing sort of partial swimming where I pushed off the bottom within my depth and flailed wildly for a few strokes. The bubby pool had places where I was out of my depth out near the chain, and Mum would have seen me making little forays under it into the big pool. I was close to being able to swim and loved playing in the water and would pester her relentlessly to take me to the baths.

Not long after my gutter swimming adventure, Mum decided it would be a good idea for me to get my 'Herald'. Each summer, The Herald newspaper sponsored a 'Learn to Swim' programme with a certificate, 'The Herald', as a reward for being able to swim twenty-five yards. This particular year, the programme took place at the Bendigo East Baths, another sandy-bottomed, concrete-walled swimming pool that was filled with water in early summer and topped up at intervals. No chlorine, just water!

I went to a couple of lessons in the afternoons with a lot of children I didn't know. A man stood on the edge showing us how to turn our heads and breathe on the side and keep our arm strokes going. Soon I was able to swim the distance fairly easily and we learnt that there was to be a big night of testing for the certificates.

One hot night after dinner, when it was getting dark, Mum drove me to the pool. As we got near, we could see lights on poles shining through the night. We found the Herald people gathering us up at the deep end. We had been taught at the shallow end, and by now I was getting nervous. I'd never swum in the dark and this was all different.

The water looked black, and the lights glinted on the little waves kicked up by all the people playing and diving from the nearby spring boards. I was told I had to swim along the edge to down 'there', but I couldn't really tell where 'there' was. There were so many people around and such a lot of shouting. I didn't feel like doing this but got into the line of kids anyway.

Then it was my turn. I jumped into the dark water, came up and started to swim off down the pool. Fierce yellow lights glared in my eyes and waves of dark water buffeted me and upset my breathing. I was frightened and confused, got a mouthful of water, coughed and grazed up against the rough concrete side wall. I stopped and hung onto it. People leant over me trying to persuade me to keep going. Even Mum came across. Still, I refused to go further and climbed out.

I never did get my Herald. On the other hand, I had learnt enough to swim happily and confidently and soon Mum would let me go down to the baths by myself.

I loved playing in the water, which was like a playground where I could jump and land without a thud. I'd run down the banks of the big pool and leap into the water. My fall was cushioned and I would allow myself to float to the bottom in a coating of bubbles and then push up off the sand to burst through the surface into the air. I learnt to surge off underwater from the wall and see how far I could get, pretending to be a fish.

I tried to dive from the side but could only do belly whacker after belly whacker till someone's dad said, 'Keep your head down!' That worked.

A group would get together and play 'keepings off' with a tennis ball, or we would create a seething mass of slippery kids all trying to duck each other. You'd jump with your hands on someone's shoulders and try to push them under. Then you'd let go and they'd be on the hunt to duck you.

In addition to just playing, I found that my body moved well in the water. I liked the weightlessness and being able to float and 'fly' in and through this watery medium.

I swam my teenage summers away with the discipline of training twice a day, following the black line on the bottom of the new Bendigo Olympic Pool, using my muscles and energy. I enjoyed the contrast between the isolation of swimming and the fun of sitting around with my club friends, eating ice creams, laughing and joking and mucking around.

Now, I go through stages of swimming laps for fitness but find it boring, especially as it's mostly in an indoor pool and I need to wear goggles, which I never did as a kid. My eyes never got sore then.

Swimming freely in the sea or a river or a lake is completely different.

The heaviness of living on land is forgotten as I lie in the water which embraces and supports me. I am light and floating and move languidly. The water creeps all over my body: between my toes, between my legs, under my arms and over my scalp, cooling my hot head. My ears and nostrils allow in just a little water.

I still enjoy the 'dead man's float', lying spreadeagled on my back, head relaxed and toes bobbing through the surface of the water, the water in my ears blocking and muffling sounds till I hear only trickles. Ripples lap against my body and I go where the water takes me.

In the sea, the 'dead man's float' allows a gentle swell to lift and release my body. I think of what it would be like as a baby to sleep in my mother's arms. The words 'lying on the bosom of the sea' rise to the surface of my mind and make me feel safe and embraced. Poets and writers have written about 'the bosom of the sea' for centuries, and I must have picked up the phrase from somewhere and added the 'lying on' concept for my own contentment.

I am alone and free, yet supported.

Chapter Two
Eaglehawk

Eaglehawk in the 1950s was the sort of place where a kid could roam around playing where she wanted. She could ride her bike down to the unpatrolled baths in the park or walk up to the shops to buy comics and lollies.

Growing up, I loved the idea of 'Eaglehawk'. I would search the sky for the soaring wedge-tailed eagle after which our gold mining town was named. The name seemed too magnificent for the shabby little town of single-storey weatherboard miners' cottages which huddled and sprawled behind the tall brick churches, banks and scary, noisy pubs on the main road. The double-storey town hall, down at the tram terminus, was defended by two brown, shiny cannons facing up the street. We kids played on them while our mums were in the small post office tucked under the skirts of the town hall's ornate façade.

The grown-ups told me there were still gold reefs and mine tunnels lying underneath our streets. They said that a hundred years ago there had been forty thousand people living in Eaglehawk. In one way, I could believe this because the town seemed empty, as if its clothes were too big for it, but on the other hand, it was hard to imagine what it would have been like with all those people around.

Our little town was low and flat, lying under a big sky like an island surrounded by grey-green bush, but tethered by the tram line to the large town of Bendigo, four miles away. The tram ran down High Street, which we all called the main road or 'up the street'. It was the only asphalted street in town, and the spinal cord of the tram tracks running down its centre meant that a dark green tram could suddenly appear amongst the sparse traffic and ring its bell at a car or bike behaving vaguely. The ribs running from the main road spine were the wide gravel streets I knew best: Haggar, Church, Victoria and Napier. There weren't many cars around and the streets were empty and safe to play and ride on.

Church Street, where we lived, was wide and unsealed so the tyres of passing cars made a deep crunching sound on the gravel. Our house was on the inner side of a curve, and cars tended to take the direct line on our side, which left quite a wide bit of open roadside for us all to play on, just in front of Wowo and Wally's house opposite us.

As a small child, my explorations started from the front verandah of our big red-brick house with its cast-iron lace fringe. It was an upright Edwardian house with a sense of being corseted and a bit supervisory of the low weatherboard houses opposite. These houses had their own personalities. Some sank low into the ground like chooks having a dust bath, looking exhausted behind their faded paint and unused verandahs; others stood high and crisp with a few steps up to their front verandahs which faced neat lawns and flower beds. All houses had red corrugated iron roofs, front gardens behind the fence and a large backyard where the real things happened.

I knew who lived in each house. One had the scary brown dog with the yellow eyes; others had the old people we hardly ever saw. But the best ones were those with children in them. Next door to us was a big brick house like ours, lived in by an old couple who didn't say much to anyone. Later, I learnt that the few brick houses in Eaglehawk had been built by the mine owners.

There seemed to be as many peppercorn trees around as there were gum trees. The house on the corner had a row of tall rounded pepper trees overhanging the footpath, making a shady place to play. The old mines and sand dumps were surrounded by pepper trees, and all school yards had a few, also making shady spots. I liked the soft, pungent, drooping fronds and the little pink peppercorns that appeared each year and dropped to the ground for us to crunch underfoot. Apparently, they'd been introduced from Peru as an ornamental tree and had gone wild.

As an adult, I'm amazed at how, in the space of about fifty years from the 1850s to the turn of the century, a churned-up landscape of gullies, raw clay pits, heaps of dirt, tents and cooking fires had been transformed into an organised township. Gold panning and individual prospecting had transitioned to employment in deep mines. There were planned streets, drainage, electricity, shops, banks, pubs, schools, churches, a police station and lock-up, a formal cemetery, a town hall for the local council, a Mechanics Institute to educate the miners, an excavated lake with a rowing club, and swimming baths. This transformation was achieved through an incredible surge of optimism and money from gold. It was when the gold became inaccessible, even in the deep mines, that the town lost its energy.

Our street flowed down from the hill near the cemetery and became my playground from about the time I was five. Kids from up and down the road would appear out of their front gates on their bikes, or with their footies, or the latest toy, all drifting together to play.

Street games came and went according to unknown signals. One of these signals had all the kids on the street walking around on jam or golden syrup tins with string loops attached for our hands to hold them firm. I had seen a man walking on real tall stilts in the Bendigo Easter Procession and desperately wanted some. I asked and asked everyone, and eventually Wally said he would make some for me. I had a long wait for Wally's stilts. Finally, Mum told me that Wally had said that they were ready, so I raced across the road and around the side of their house and there they were, standing against Wally's sofa on the back verandah.

But? What were these? There were two long bits of building wood with a sort of triangular step screwed to each one, about a foot from the ground. In my mind, stilts hadn't looked like this. Had I really thought that I would strap long poles onto my shoes and just head off? I don't know. But I was disappointed and confused by these things. I couldn't see what you did with them.

But Wowo and Wally knew. Wally stood them up in front of me. Wowo stood behind me and told me to place my foot on one step, lean forward and tuck the long support behind my shoulder and then hold it where my hand fell. Aah! She held me steady. I stepped onto the other one and sorted out my arms and grip. Now I could see how they worked. I could balance and work my legs and arms together to take steps. Wowo helped me for a while, and I found that if I kept my weight forward, I could walk and also just step off to the front if I got wobbly. Very soon, I got the knack.

I loved those stilts. I could stride down our drive and onto the footpath and walk up and down. I could run with them but couldn't quite jump. Soon, another pair appeared on the street. Someone's father had got busy. It was fun to go walking around together for a while. But then the craze just faded away. The stilts were propped against the garage wall, waiting for another time.

Bows and arrows also came and went. Making these was a bit of a group effort. We all knew that bamboo was best for the bows because it bent so well. Suddenly, the kids who had a big clump of bamboo in the middle of their chook yard were under a bit of pressure. Their parents didn't like us going into the chook yard and said there were snakes in the bamboo patch. We didn't know whether to believe that or not, but when their mum was out shopping, we invaded the chooks and came out with some tall bits of smooth bamboo which we took back to our place to turn into bows. Arrows were a problem, and it was good if we could scrounge some thin bits of dowel from someone's shed. We knew we shouldn't shoot at each other and usually didn't.

When there were a lot of us around, we could play a good game of dodgie out on the road. It was best to play dodgie with a basketball or a big rubber ball, but you could do it with a tennis ball. That became faster and scarier and dangerously near a confined sort of Poison Ball. The gravel meant that the rectangle could be marked out easily and dodgie brought out some girls. In all the other games, it was usually just me and the boys, most of whom were a bit younger than I was. Actually, I was probably the oldest kid playing in the street but never thought of it like that at the time.

Some games were clearly seasonal; cricket gave way to footie which gave way to cricket again. I never thought about why these changes happened, but I think they must have generated from the football-loving families in the street. It was time to get the footie out when the footie season started. It was always Australian Rules; we hadn't even heard of soccer or rugby!

A group would coalesce and a footie would appear. We would

play Kick to Kick (kicking the ball from one end to the other) which could be with only me and my brother Richard, but sometimes we might have about three or four boys on each end and we'd race to catch the 'mark' and a chance to kick. The ball was usually old and bloated, but when it was pumped up properly, it gave a terrific tight 'ping' when you kicked it.

The road sloped gently towards the gutter which always had drain water in it. If the ball dribbled towards the gutter, we'd run hard to beat it to the water which was not only wet, obviously, but smelly. A ball resting soggily in the gutter was not attractive, but we'd just pick it up and continue the game, trying not to take a mark on our chests for a while. Our jumpers must have ended up stinking and wet, but I don't remember Mum ever complaining about having to wash them.

At school, the boys were gradually being taught how to play Aussie Rules properly. They taught me how to handball and do a punt kick and a drop kick. I loved jostling and leaping for a mark and then running out to kick back to the other end. There was never a remote chance that I'd be able to play proper games in a team down at the Eaglehawk Football Ground like Richie did later, and, actually, I never even thought of that as a possibility.

I now look at the development of the women's league playing Australian Rules, and I'm still not used to seeing women with their pony tails and mouth guards playing as hard a contact game as the men. I watched the first match on TV and wept to see the freedom these young women now have.

The street cricket season probably started during the summer school holidays. Again, there'd be the coalescence of enough kids to play, and someone would have a bat and a tennis ball, and we'd bring something for the wickets. We'd find a bit of the road where the gravel wasn't too loose and set up there. The game would nearly always be 'tippity run' – meaning you'd have to run no matter what sort of stroke you hit. That was good fun and kept the game moving. If you hit into someone's garden, you were very honourably 'out for 6'. It was far less honourable, but still 'out', if you hit into Wowo and Wally's, just ten yards to the side. The same problem of the soggy ball in the gutter existed, but less so in the drier hotter weather.

I loved batting and was usually quite hard to get out. We allowed ourselves to bowl under-arm if we wanted but would try over-arm, 'proper' bowling. We were very strict on throwing. This made it hard for all of us, and I never learnt to bowl satisfyingly. Again, there was no official cricket for girls, but I didn't mind too much because the thought of standing around fielding in the sun for hours on a hot afternoon was pretty unappealing. Batting would have been alright, but the pool was much better.

There was no problem with traffic simply because there was hardly any. Whoever saw a car coming would yell out, 'Car!' and we'd just draw off the road for a moment.

Parental surveillance was not an issue either; adults never came out to watch or coach. Unlike nowadays, our parents just let us get on with it without feeling the need to know every little thing we did or wanting to improve us. We just played.

Sometimes, a game on the road would be interrupted by the horse and cart that came to sell greengroceries. We'd see the horse coming down the street, pulling the flat cart covered in boxes of vegetables and fruit, and would go racing in to tell our mothers. They'd come down their driveways and gather around the cart to do their shopping. The horse might be given a nosebag to harrumph and chew in whilst the greengrocer weighed and packed for the mothers. He had a shiny old leather bag around his waist to put the money in.

Early on, we had an ice-chest for our milk, butter and meat. The problem with that was that the ice melted. We weren't meant to open the top bit to look at the big new block of ice or, worse, to see how much had melted later in the week. But I would, just to look at such a large piece of ice. A big van would come down the road, and we'd crowd around to watch the driver open the back door. I loved the wave of cold air flowing out and the sight of all the stacked-up ice. He had a sack over his left shoulder and used a big hook to drag out a gleaming, translucent block, sling it on his shoulder and do a sort of running-walk up the drive to put it into our ice-chest. Often, he'd give us chips of ice to suck, and we'd juggle the piece from hand to hand as we crunched it up. Once, I got a piece too big to eat. It was about the size of a jagged grapefruit with shining angled facets, and I could see bands of bubbles trapped inside. I got a tea towel to hold it in while it gradually melted, and I licked its coldness while admiring its beauty.

We had a big gate in our back fence which opened into a different sort of place. Instead of a house, there was a big empty hall, which used to be a mattress factory. Just like our house, it was made of red bricks, but it had no front fence. A long broken-down shed stood along the side fence. Mum said that it used to be stables for horses to live in. Now there were only spiders living in thick clumps of dusty web. We could walk between the hall and the shed to reach the back street.

One day when I was out riding around the back street, I saw that the front door of the building was open and that a car was parked in the yard. That was strange. I rode home, noticed that our back gate was shut and peeped through the fence. I couldn't see anything different. Mum said that she thought a family had moved in. We saw a light in their back window that night.

A few days later, I rode by with Jane and Richie to have a sticky beak. The big front doors were open, and inside the front bit was a deep hole in the floor and ground with a car over it and a whole lot of tools lying around.

A man in blue overalls said, 'G'day,' and went down into the hole and started banging things on the bottom of the car. There were some kids in the yard, and we stood and looked at each other for a while before doing a bit of talking. We played with them a bit. A few days later, while playing again, it started to rain so they said, 'Do you wanna come inside?' That was a bit unusual because we didn't usually go into each other's houses unless we were best friends.

We followed them through a door behind the front workshop into the huge hall. The floor was rough concrete and the brick walls patchy with faded paint. There were mattresses on the floor made up into beds, and piles of clothes lay around. A saggy, faded couch and chairs in the far corner was their lounge room. The centre of the room was empty, so we started running around playing chasey. Their mother came out of a little door from the small narrow kitchen at the back. She looked tired and cross.

'Who are these children? I didn't say you could bring anyone in.'

I felt that she was embarrassed, and that made us embarrassed too. We said we lived 'there' and pointed to our house, said goodbye and left.

We were shocked to see a family living like that. One day, they were just gone. Mum said that she thought that his car repair business didn't go too well.

If you turned right from our driveway, you went up the hill to the top end of the road. Our house was actually in a gentle valley as the road sloped down from the Main Road, crossed the little covered drain near us, which flowed towards Eaglehawk Creek, and then rose again towards the cemetery. It was fun to have a hill to race down on our bikes. We'd line up at the top and then pedal breathlessly down, over the corrugations, watching the side street on the left and then on to our corner.

There was a seasonal craze for billy carts, and anyone who had one would be out and about in their own dad-constructed creation. A lot of billy cart playing involved running and pushing, so each seat had to have a raised back rest for the pusher to hold on to as he or she pushed the driver. Otherwise you pushed the driver's back. The hill was good because you could play by yourself. You just pulled the cart up and then set off to jolt down the road rather frighteningly.

Despite being very good at jam and marmalade, our Dad didn't build things, and for a long time we were envious of all the other kids' billy carts. Making a billy cart seemed a bit tricky, and although I could see what I'd have to do, I didn't know how to actually do it. You needed old pram wheels and the wood to be sawn up just right. The other tricky part was the loose bolt that had to be screwed to the central board between the front and back axles, which allowed you to steer. It was beyond me. But somehow, our family did get one. I can't remember how that happened. Did I ask Wally to make it? Did Mum ask Wally to make it? Who else would make one for us? Was it more my brother's than mine? At the end of the craze, the billy cart would go into the garage to join the stilts.

We'd play with our bikes quite a lot. My sister and brother

had been given new, shiny coloured bikes, but I was still riding Mum's faded old one. I'm not sure why I never got given a new one, despite this bike being huge and heavy. We'd race and play 'chicken' and see who could make the longest skid. At times, we'd make our bikes buzz like a motorbike by pegging swap cards to the strut of the back wheel so that they riffled across the spokes.

One afternoon, when I was about eight or nine, everyone had gone home. I was riding in circles down near the pepper trees on the corner and wondering what to do next when a big group of boys on bikes came flying down Church Street and swooped around the corner. They saw me, stopped, said something to each other and turned around to ride up to me. The biggest one said, 'We're going down to look at something at the park. Do want to come?'

'Alright.' That was a bit surprising. It was nice to be asked.

So off we went, doing that pedalling thing where you're trying hard not to look as if you're trying but are really going as fast as you possibly can. We surged into the park past the croquet club, swung right and skidded to a stop in front of the weatherboard baths' change rooms. It was an autumn afternoon, and no one was swimming or at the playground.

'It's in here', they said, going into the ladies change room.

That seemed funny, boys going into the ladies', but I went in there with them. The room was empty: no clothing hanging from the hooks and no neatly rolled-up bundles of clothes on the wooden benches. Not even a neat little pile of boy poo on the floor waiting to disgust us.

'What is it?'

They stood around me, a bit shy and jostling and nudging each other.

'Lie down on the floor and we'll show you.'

I could have stopped there but didn't. I was curious and at the same time aware that I probably shouldn't be doing this.

I lay on the centre of the floor. The boards were dusty.

'You go first', said the biggest boy, who was about eleven or twelve, to one of the little ones.

They giggled and shuffled, and the boy came over to me and lay down on top of me, each of us fully dressed. He lay there for a little while and then got told to get off. Another boy came and did the same and then another. They were very polite and a bit embarrassed, and the point seemed to be to just lie on me.

After a while, I got a bit bored, and so, between boys, I got to my feet and said, 'I'm going home now.' I walked to the door. They stood back for me and I left.

I rode home feeling a bit strange and confused. I felt I had done something wrong and thought it probably had to do with this thing called 'intercourse', which I knew about. I also knew that I had chosen to go along with the boys. But then, nothing much had happened; I hadn't felt frightened and I had stopped when I wanted to. I went home for tea and never said anything to anyone about it.

My freely roaming Eaglehawk childhood quite often presented me with important choices where I had to learn to deal with the consequences of my decisions, a bit like a 'Choose Your Own Adventure' book.

If I had said no to the boys when they asked me to go with

them, that decision would have sent me home to play safely in the garden. But having said yes, I was committed to something a bit unknown and unpredictable. It could have got nasty but there was no sense of that at any stage. I left when I wanted, my curiosity satisfied.

I think that being strong and energetic gave me the confidence to start and stop things when I wanted. This probably helped as it meant my body language was also clear and decisive. All in all, it was a good lesson in saying no.

Underlying all my playing was my fundamental choice that I wanted to play like a boy with the boys. Eaglehawk allowed me to do this.

Chapter Three
Starting Out

Mum and Dad weren't from Eaglehawk, and for Mum particularly, the small, shabby town must have seemed an unlikely place to land up in. She had been born in Christchurch, New Zealand, and her family moved to Sydney when she was about nine. Her father was a bank manager in the Bank of New South Wales (now Westpac), and they later moved to Canberra and then to Launceston in Tasmania, always living above the bank. Dad was born in Melbourne, and that was where he went to school and university.

However, once established in our own house in Eaglehawk (I was two by then), they didn't move. Dad died in the Bendigo hospital in 2000, and seven years later, Mum moved to a retirement village in Melbourne, where Sally, my youngest sister, and I were living. She told me then that she had always been expecting Dad to tell her that they would be moving somewhere else. Fifty-nine years in the one house had apparently been an ongoing astonishment to her.

Mum and I lived with her parents for the first two years of my life because my father was caught up in the aftermath of the war. Mum had also been living with them during her pregnancy with me, her first child, while Dad was away in the army. By now, her father was the Manager of the Bank of New South Wales in Bendigo, and we all lived in the flat above the bank. We were in View Street, opposite Rosalind Park with its large heavy-foliaged elms, and near Alexandra Fountain at the centre of the main crossroads. Originally called Sandhurst Town, Bendigo is a handsome gold rush city, graced with ornate Victorian public buildings, which can be seen in one its oldest streets, Pall Mall. From the bank's windows, you could see the tower of the post office and hear its clock chiming every quarter hour. I learnt much later that they were the Big Ben chimes.

I was born in 1945 on a very hot December Saturday afternoon at the Bendigo Base Hospital. It seems that I had presented myself in the breech position, and there was a bit of a stalemate. The doctor made the decision to dislocate my knee to enable the delivery. Apparently, that did the trick and I was delivered, safe and sound, only needing my knee to be 'put back'.

Mum enjoyed telling the sequel to this story, which occurred about six weeks later when she was out shopping in Pall Mall with me in my pram.

Coming the other way was the doctor who had delivered me. He greeted Mum and, without much small talk, bent over the pram, peeled off the blanket and lifted my leg (Mum can't remember which one) and twisted it around.

'That's good,' he said. 'I was a bit worried about it.'

He moved on, leaving Mum to tuck me back in. I still don't know which knee it was; both of them always seemed fine!

My first memory is of being on the open steps of a high wooden staircase leading down to a garden. I had crawled down backwards but was now frozen with fear. I could see through the gaps and knew I was up in the air and barely supported. I was too frightened to move up or down and felt that I could easily slide through a gap and fall to the ground.

I carefully lifted my eyes from the grey wooden step in front of me and looked up at the grown-ups. Mum, her visiting brother, Gordon, and Nana and Da were basking in deck chairs on the wooden deck outside the kitchen, where we'd been sitting. They were all looking at me, saying things to each other and laughing a bit. No one got up to help me. Finally, I carefully reached out a hand to the next step up and kneed myself on to it and then did the same on to the next one, slow and frightened, until I could crawl on to the level deck. There, I was humiliated and confused by the laughter and noise which greeted me.

I had been lonely and afraid, stuck down there on those stairs. No one understood that I was frightened. I needed a grown-up to pick me up and help me feel safe. I know that I managed to rescue myself, but it felt too hard.

Dad must have visited us at intervals, because my new sister, Jane, was born when I was twenty-three months old. Soon after that, our family – Dad now living with us – moved to our own house in Eaglehawk.

On Sundays, we sometimes visited Nana and Da for afternoon tea. The adults would sit in the brown leather armchairs and drink tea out of clattering cups and saucers. I would be allowed to have a bit of cake. I liked those visits.

We would also go into Bendigo for special shopping. One day, Mum, Jane in her pusher and I were there to buy me a jumper at The Beehive, a big shop selling all sorts of things. Mum took me to a counter with a lady standing behind it and a tall chair in front of it.

'I'm looking for a jumper for this one,' she said pointing at me.

They looked down at me, decided what size I was and then

talked a bit about jumpers. I watched from the tall chair, onto which I'd now climbed up. The lady, who was dressed all in black, turned to the wooden drawers set in the wall behind her and lifted out a few jumpers, which she put on the counter for us to look at. When we'd chosen one and I'd tried it on, the lady wrote something on a little pad, tore off the sheet, took Mum's money and put both into a metal cylinder, which she fitted into a hissing tube behind her. It went *whoomph* and got sucked away and then went whizzing off on wires up near the ceiling.

'What's that?' I asked, amazed by the elaborate wires and whooshing.

Mum told me that it went up to an office where ladies took out the money and the docket, put the change and a receipt back in and whizzed it back down to us. We waited for the arriving *whoomph* at our end, were handed our receipt and parcel and left, heading back to Pall Mall and the car.

Suddenly, there were the toys! I stopped short! Right at my height sat a large golden teddy bear who looked at me with his kind eyes and broad friendly face. He seemed to smile. His arms reached towards me, and I wanted him more than I had ever wanted anything before.

'Mum! Look! Can I have him?'

'No, I don't think so. We have to get back to the car.' She walked on.

'But I want him!'

I'd lifted him off the shelf and was hugging his big round body and feeling his soft fur against my face. He felt so loving and kind.

'No. We've got to get home. Put it back.'

'Nooo! I want him. Pleeese.'

'No, Elizabeth, you can't have everything you want. Now just come!'

My eyes got watery. I didn't want to leave the bear behind. I was sad and desperate and started to cry a bit. Then I remembered tantrums, which I'd seen other children do, and thought I would try to do one. I started some very loud crying. Mum looked around to see who was watching. My sister, Jane, started crying too. Amongst the tears, I had a little thought that I could try lying on the floor and kicking. I was just about to do that when …

'All right, Elizabeth. I'll put it on lay-by, but it will have to be your Christmas present.'

Happiness flooded me. In a flash, I stopped crying.

'Thank you, Mummy.'

It was a good choice to put on the tantrum, and Mum made a good decision to indulge me.

I was usually a 'good' child who didn't make a fuss about things, but now as an adult, I think that I found it a bit hard at times and wanted more comfort and softness than I got. When I saw that bear, I knew I had to have him. He could be kind and comforting for me. He was too big to take to bed, but just seeing him sitting on a chair in the bedroom was comfort enough. I've loved Teddy all my life and still have him.

Teddy had a 'renovation' a few years ago by a teddy bear restorer. She unpicked his panels of golden fur and washed them and removed his moth-egg-infested stuffing and broken 'growl'. She completely re-stuffed him, gave him a new growl, sewed on new suede paws and replaced swivels so that his arms, legs and head could move again. He still looks very handsome and sits on a bookshelf in our bedroom where I see him smiling at me every morning.

When I was three and eight months, I had to sleep at the bank by myself. I know now that Mum was in hospital having had my brother (but where was my sister?). Da, my grandfather, was looking after me because Nana couldn't. She wore a sort of iron frame on her leg and had to use a walking stick all the time. Her face was stiff on one side, and her lipstick would get dribbly. Mum said that was because she had had strokes. Her white hair was always in waves like lines around her head and she wasn't really very friendly towards me. I was a bit scared of her.

When I was tucked up in bed that first night, Da put a small hand bell on my bedside table.

'When you wake up in the morning, you can come into my bedroom and ring this bell. Goodnight, Elizabeth.'

I was entranced by the little silver bell, so when I woke up, I walked along the dark hall to his bedroom, crept in, stood beside his bed and saw the back of his head, which was on about the same level as mine. I lifted my arm and tentatively rang the bell. He stirred and heaved around and looked at me in the half dark.

'Oh, it's still dark. It's far too early. Go back to bed.' He slumped back down on to his pillow.

I was confused and disappointed. I'd done it wrongly. I went back to bed and waited until I heard him get up and it would be safe for me to come out.

After breakfast, Dad came and took me in the car on a long, long drive to stay with his sister Doff while Mum was still in hospital. 'Doff' was the best shot I could make of Dorothy. I didn't really know her or George, her husband. They didn't have any children, and the two of them lived in a little house built on top of the sloping roof of a huge square building by a river.

The building was the Richmond Electricity Terminal Station,

where the electricity coming in from the power stations of the Latrobe Valley about 150 miles away was distributed to some of Melbourne's suburbs. I learnt much later that George was their chief engineer.

That first time, Dad must have left me there and gone home. I don't remember making a fuss; it just seemed to happen. There was a small bedroom just for me, and on top of the brown wardrobe was a large, round leather case that contained a drum, which I somehow knew about. It wasn't as big as the ones the marching drummers carried across their stomachs at the Bendigo Easter Procession; but it was one of those that sat a bit sideways across their hips. Somehow, I connected the drum with George being a Scotchie and knew it meant he would dress up in those special clothes, with a kilt, and play that drum. I longed to see him dressed up and carrying his drum. He was very big and dark, and I wanted to see him looking huge and magnificent in their small, neat drawing room up there in the sky. I asked Doff very politely if I could see him in his band clothes. She didn't seem to answer the question, and although I waited, I never saw George dressed up.

What was more normal and like home was that we listened to *Kindergarten of the Air* on the radio. I sat on the carpet and Doff in a chair nearby. She knew the songs, which surprised me, and we sang them together.

Doff read stories to me, and I particularly liked the way she read *Puss in Boots* with really good voices for the characters. I heard that the cat *minced* in his boots.

'What is *minced*?' I asked.

Doff stood up and walked in tiny, neat steps across the room. I could just imagine the cat doing that in his thigh-high boots and loved seeing Doff being the cat for me.

Later on, Mum told me that Doff wrote stories for '*Kindergarten of the Air*'. I wish I'd known what they were and had them read to me.

One evening, I was having my bath, sitting and splashing about a bit, when suddenly the door opened and in came Doff. She said hello, went to the toilet at the end of the bath, pulled her skirt up, sat and did wee with the most tremendous noise, wiped herself, flushed the toilet, straightened her clothes, washed her hands and left, closing the door again.

I was astonished! I had never seen a grown-up go to the toilet before and wasn't even all that used to flushing inside toilets. And she did seem rather close. At home at Eaglehawk, we still had a lav in a little weatherboard house out in the backyard, where you sat on a bench with a hole in it above a big metal pan. Rude people called it a dunny. Nana and Da had an inside flushing one. I still used a potty a lot of the time because I didn't like going to the dunny.

What was even more interesting and exciting was the way Doff and George's shopping was hauled up to their rooftop house, and how the rubbish bins went down. Their house had a sort of asphalt space between it and the safety walls. On one end of the roof was a metal pole with a cross arm, some wheels and rope and a winding handle. I watched George attach the rubbish bin to this somehow. Then he swung the arm over the outside and wound the handle, which let the bin go down and down until it reached the ground a long way below. I was allowed to lean out to watch if someone held me. The shopping came up like this too, but then he had to turn the handle round the opposite way.

On the other end of the roof, George took me to look over the wall at a deep pool separated from the river behind it. He lifted me up and asked if I could see a big yellow fish down there. I looked and looked but couldn't see it in the brown water. I was frustrated and disappointed not to be able to see the fish.

That was my first visit to Doff and George's. Considering that I was so young, I'm surprised that I was so content to be there. But then, when I think about it, I realise that I was there on my own, without a baby sister taking Mum's time. It was quiet and peaceful, and I got a lot of attention.

Dad must have collected me and travelled the hundred miles back to Eaglehawk, but I don't remember the journey at all. Maybe, I slept.

My first memory of the new baby is of us all sitting in the sun on the side verandah. Mum and the baby had come home. The baby was a boy called Richard. Nana and Da were visiting, and there were teacups and cake on the little table. I looked up at my little brother's bassinet with the white net trailing over it and remembered something that had happened a long time ago.

I was standing beside Mum's bed. It was daytime, and she was still in bed. My head only came up to about the top of the mattress so I had to look up at Mum as she lay there with a lot of pillows under her head.

'Mummy, why are you in bed?'

She told me that she was unwell and that the baby growing inside her might not be able to see or hear when it was born because of this sickness.

'Oh!'

I hadn't liked the idea of that.

Now, on the verandah, I suddenly needed to know and asked

Mum, 'Are his eyes all right? Can he see? Can he hear us?'

The adults did a sort of snorting, laughing noise and all looked at each other and me. I felt as if I'd said something wrong.

'Yes, darling. He's fine. He's a beautiful baby boy.' Mum looked surprised.

'You were sick and you told me he might not be able to see.'

I was glad that he was all right. They all started talking and pouring more tea.

I'm guessing that it must have been German measles that had sent Mum to bed in her early pregnancy. It had felt a bit like a secret when she told me that the baby might not be able to see or hear. I was three and didn't really want to be involved in Mum's worry.

Wowo and Wally lived directly across the road from us. I couldn't say *Mr and Mrs Wallace*, so *Wowo and Wally* it became. Even though one says *Mr and Mrs* in that order, it was the reverse for me: Wowo was Mrs Wallace. They were older than Mum and Dad, and they had never had any children in their small, white weatherboard house. I would talk to them over their front fence with Mum, and gradually it seemed alright to go over the road by myself.

One summer evening, when I was quite little, I decided to visit them. I crept out of bed and out the front door, crossed the road, which, as usual, didn't have a car in sight. I quietly opened their front gate, walked around the side to the back and surprised them in their kitchen. They had had dinner and were sitting reading the paper.

'Oh, Elizabeth! What are you doing here?' Wowo exclaimed, both pushing their chairs back and standing up.

'I thought I'd come and see you,' I answered.

'But shouldn't you be in bed?'

'Yes, but I wanted to come here.'

'Oh, they'll be worried. And she's just in her nightie! Wally, go and tell them she's here.'

I sat down in Wally's chair and wondered why this hadn't turned out to be a nice visit. Wowo didn't seem to know what to do. She sat in her chair and then got up and then sat down again, all the while looking at me.

Mum came over to get me. I heard Wally say to Wowo that Mum and Dad hadn't noticed I'd gone. I don't think they were cross with me. On hindsight, I suppose that I'd been put to bed but on such a hot, light night, I didn't feel like sleeping and just slipped out through the front fly-wire door for a bit of an adventure.

That misadventure didn't stop me visiting, and I would often go over the road to see them when I wanted a bit of company and couldn't find anything to do.

It was always comforting over at Wowo and Wally's. I loved their house because it was small and so different from our big one. They had a bedroom on one side of the front door with a huge high double bed in it. The other side of the front door was the 'good room', which I don't think I ever sat in. The front windows were covered in thick white lacy curtains. No one used the front door.

The back was the best because of the cosy, friendly kitchen. A black wood-burning stove against the outside wall of the room made it warm and comfortable in winter. It was hot in summer, but Wowo was really good at having just the amount of heat she needed to cook with. Wally's job was to keep the split wood supply ready for her, and he would come in from outside with a big armful of wood for the wood box down beside the stove. I loved seeing the warm orange fire when she lifted off the heavy circular covers with a special tool that hooked into them. I was never allowed to put in the wood though. As well as normal cooking, Wowo would boil up milk to make a sort of lumpy cream. It was delicious.

In front of the back window was a big table, but perhaps it was big only in proportion to the room. It was always covered with a shiny sort of tablecloth, which Wowo wiped clean with a wet cloth. We had tablecloths but Mum had to wash them. Wally's chair was tucked in the corner, side on to the window, and Wowo sat at the long edge of the table in front of the window.

At meal times (I sometimes still seemed to be there), she would get up and down a bit to poke the stove and perhaps give Wally a second helping of vegetables from the saucepans keeping warm at the back. Sometimes, I was allowed to sit with them and I sat on Wowo's left side. I would have a slice of white bread and butter and a glass of milk in a Vegemite glass with a coloured picture on it. They would offer me tea, but I didn't like it.

There was a big dresser on the back wall that had all their plates and bowls and cups on it. On each side of the fireplace, flowery curtains hung to hide the shelves. To the right, Wowo kept food and to the left were the saucepans and cake tins.

In winter, the room was a bit dark until the end of the afternoon when the westerly sun shone in. I loved sitting in the glow of both the sun and the fire.

Opening off the kitchen was a small room with a single bed in it. I slept in it one night when I was older. I can't remember why I was there but felt a bit shy and embarrassed because of the fuss they made of me.

I liked Wowo's laundry. You went down a passage to the left of the back door and straight into it. At our place, you had to go outside the back door to get to our laundry, which seemed cold and full of hard things compared to Wowo's. They had wallpapered the passage and the laundry into a bright patchwork of coloured pictures and headlines with pages cut from magazines and sometimes even newspapers. There were quite a lot of horses because Wally liked the races. They were stuck on with glue called Clag. It was exciting to look at their walls, which made the big room, a sort of lean-to, friendly and bright. Wowo had a wood-fired copper to boil up the washing, just like Mum's.

Wowo made good Clag out of flour and water which she cooked on her stove until it became clear and thin like the official Clag you could buy at the newsagent in a conical jar with a built-in brush in the lid. I tried to make Clag like that at home the next time I wanted some, but it didn't work. I ended with the same lumpy, white Clag we always made.

Wally's empire was on the back verandah, which was always sunny in the afternoon. He had a sort of wooden couch against the kitchen wall. There were a couple of flat cushions and he used to sit there and smoke. I liked to sit next to him, and sometimes we would talk and sometimes we wouldn't. I enjoyed watching him roll his cigarettes from little bits of paper from a special packet and curly, fresh-smelling tobacco he would take out of a blue sort of envelope made of strong, shiny paper. This was much more interesting than Dad's cigarettes which were already rolled up in a little cardboard box. I liked watching the way the tube of tobacco and paper could be sealed by a lick of Wally's tongue along the edge. Then I'd watch the paper flare a bit as it caught from the match. Wally had a special way of holding the lit match to the end of the cigarette in his cupped hands. He had to strike the match and then quickly get it up to the shelter of the other hand and at the same time suck the cigarette to make the fire light the tobacco. Then he'd sit back and blow out the smoke.

I sat there with him in the quiet afternoon sun. It felt peaceful and friendly.

Wally was a small, neat man, compared to his broad, buxom wife. When I was little, he would head off early in the morning on his bike to work at the Ordinance Factory. The bike had a sort of sling bag for his lunch made from a hessian sack hanging from the cross bar. There would be quite a lot of Eaglehawk men leaving on their bikes to go to work, either at the big, white Ordinance Factory off the back road into Bendigo or at the Bendigo Railway Workshops. There was an early morning siren blaring over the town to make sure these workers got off to work on time. I would hear it while I was still in bed, and on a winter's morning, I was especially glad it wasn't me cycling off in the frosty air.

Some fathers had a little bike seat mounted on the cross bar so that they could take one of their children somewhere on the bike. I thought I'd like to sit on a little seat like that with my big father taking me safely for a ride. However, my father was famous within the family for not being able to ride a bike. I had a secret wish, which I barely admitted to myself, that Wally would get a little seat for me, but he didn't.

However, he did make a boat for me to float in the lake. It was an unusual craft, and I think Wowo was a bit embarrassed by it. It was more like a raft made of a square of quite thick yellowy wood with the corners cut to make a sort of circle with angles. Then he had nailed an opened tin can to the centre and somehow fitted a mast within it. He'd painted the can red and the whole thing was rather jaunty. I took it down to the lake, and although it did float and bob around, it was hard to know what actually to do with it.

Still, I was really happy that Wally had made it for me.

Even though I was still only about four or five, I enjoyed the freedom of getting around the streets and neighbourhood by myself. I knew the shortcuts and most of the people in one way or another.

Late one Sunday afternoon, Mum realised that we were out of honey. I had been with her to the man in the back street who sold honey before. We would take a jar with us and go to his garden shed, where he kept the honey in a big container with a tap in at the bottom. He would turn the tap on to let the honey stream out in a golden river and fill our jar. Then we would give him some money and walk home with our new honey.

'I'll go,' I said. I thought this would be fun to do by myself, so I took the jar and the money and ran out the back gate past the empty hall and down to the house with the honey in the shed. I went down their drive and up the steps to their little back porch where I knocked on their door. The man opened it. Behind him, their kitchen was all lit up and warm and smelt of food.

'Could we have some honey, please?'

'Yes, love. Brian can do that for you.'

He yelled into the house, 'Brian! Honey!'

I knew that Brian was their son. He looked like a man and was very big and a bit fat and talked in a different way, like a not very smart kid. Brian came to the door, and I followed him out to the shed.

It was a bit dark in there, and Brian turned around and said in a sort of excited voice, 'Look at what I've got,' and opened his fly. I could see the pink curve of his penis and the straggly black hair around it as he tried to tug it out through his underpants. I knew what little boys' penises looked like but did not want to be in a dark shed with that big one there at eye level.

I turned around and ran home through the twilight with my empty jar.

'Brian showed me his penis!' I shouted as I raced into our bright, busy kitchen.

'Oh dear,' said Mum, turning around from the stove with a wooden spoon in her hand.

She told Dad, and Dad said that he'd better ring the father and let him know. Dad was the doctor, and this seemed to be something he would do as part of his work. I listened to him talking on the phone but couldn't hear the words. Mum explained that there was something a bit wrong with Brian and that he didn't really mean to do it. That seemed a good explanation, but I never went to get honey again and always felt a bit funny passing their house.

It was just one of the things that happened that I sorted out for myself. I'm glad I chose to run home and not stay there too frightened to move.

By about five, I was well aware that there was something privileged about being a boy. I think I was conscious of being nudged to the edge of the family group which had my very busy mother at the centre, looking after the newest baby. I was able to entertain myself well enough, but I don't remember an adult playing with me.

Our doors never seemed to be locked, and the front gate was always open. I had a huge amount of freedom to just go out and explore and play.

Chapter Four
Getting Around

By the age of about six, I had pretty much gone as far as I could by foot around the streets near our house. I could walk up to St Peter's and the tram stop at the top of our street, to the shops, to the swimming baths and the lake and to my friends' houses. Except for rushing up to church with Mum sometimes (we always seemed to be late and rushing to places), I don't remember ever walking with a parent around these streets. I must have learnt to get around by seeing the neighbourhood from the car and then just gradually walking further and further away from home. It was perfectly natural for me to just go out the gate and go wherever I wanted.

Through the car window on our way to Bendigo, I could see that there was more of Eaglehawk to explore, like the mullock heaps and the bush, and I wanted to get out there by myself. Jane and Richard were too small to play with for long, and I had a lot of time at home with nothing much to do. I needed a bike, and by now I was too big for the trike I'd had for years. It was slow and boring, and it wouldn't take me out on to the road. I wanted to ride fast and smoothly.

So, I started looking at the dusty bike that leant against the garage wall, getting in the way of the car. It was Mum's bike, but I never saw her go anywhere on it. She told me, 'It's a war bike. They made them really heavy.' It really was very heavy and, in addition, painted a dreary maroon with 'Malvern Star' written on it in fancy writing.

Gradually, the bike became mine.

Not only was it heavy, it was huge. I could barely step across the lower fork, and the pedals, when level, were knee-high. The seat poked into my back between my shoulder blades, and the handlebars were shoulder height.

Learning to ride it was hard. Sometimes, Mum would run along behind, holding the seat, but not often enough to really let me get the feel of balancing and pedalling at the same time. I learnt to scoot along by myself with one foot on the pedal. That got me moving, and it was fun to balance. I was too scared to go from a scoot to lifting the scooting leg up over the fork to find the high pedal. I knew what I should do, but it was difficult because the bike was so big.

I took it out on to the gravel footpath where our cyclone wire fence had a wooden top at about shoulder level. I would lean the bike up against the fence as vertically as it could without falling over, stand with both feet level on the pedals and try to pedal forward hanging on to the fence with one hand. In this way, I lurched and wobbled up and down, up and down. Sometimes, I'd lean too far out and come crashing down, tangled up in the bike. My legs would be covered in chain oil, and my fence arm would get really tired.

Eventually, it worked. My surges forward became longer and more controlled, and at some stage, I could let go of the fence and keep on pedalling in more or less of a straight line. I didn't have an actual 'first ride' as the whole thing was so gradual that each stage flowed from the other until, at last, I could get the bike out, scoot, step across to the other pedal and ride straight down the drive, across the footpath, across the concrete bridge over the gutter and on to the empty road to ride wherever I wanted.

I liked to go down the couple of blocks to the lake and ride around it on the track which wound through clumps of pampas grass. There usually wasn't anyone there, and if I were alone, I would be keeping a bit of a lookout, hoping a man wouldn't appear. A busy, working sort of man was alright, but sometimes there would be a man in an old, dirty jacket and trousers, down at the park just doing nothing. I hadn't been told not to talk to strangers, but somehow I knew that these men weren't people I knew and they felt unsafe. It was bad if one of them said hello. Then I would ride on very fast.

Sometimes, it was good enough to just go down to play on the swings, which stood on tall wooden frames and had rigid bars, not chains, coming down to the seat. These bars meant that I could push up really high and not have the dropping lurch that chains gave when you went up too high for them. I loved feeling that I was tipping back with my head lower than the seat and my legs. It was fun to jump off from a high point of the swing, not the very highest, and fly through the air to land in the soft grey sand.

One morning, I messed up my landing and really hurt my left wrist, enough to make me cry. I ran home holding it and was very impressed with myself when Dad said that I'd sprained it, and then he actually bandaged it. Mum and Dad had to go down and get my abandoned bike. I felt so important going to school with a bandage on, and better still, I discovered that I could still push the school swings with my right hand. Miss Cure didn't think that was a good idea, but it was fine, and I fairly soon got sick of the bandage.

Now that I had a bike, I could ride around with the other kids in the street who had bikes. I'd ride out the drive on to the road, circle around a bit and go up and down looking up driveways, hoping that someone would come out. Often they would, and we'd go off for a bit of a ride. These kids were usually boys.

We could ride through the garden bit of the park on the smooth gravel paths and look at the flowers and the lawns. There was a shady path next to the creek with seats set in among the shrubbery, and the kids told me it was called 'lovers' lane'. We sometimes raced through it on a Sunday afternoon, giggling at the courting couples on the seats. During the week, if I were by myself, it was a bit too quiet and deserted to feel safe.

At the top of our road was the cemetery, which I liked to ride to, lean the bike against the wire side fence under the pine trees and climb through to have a bit of an explore. It didn't feel right to ride through the big front gates with the little house next to them. Often, the man who looked after the cemetery was working somewhere, and I'd try to avoid him, especially if he was digging. It was a bit horrible to think that he was digging a hole to bury a person in.

The cemetery seemed a little town set out across some small hills and criss-crossed by gravel roads and paths lined with graves, just like houses in streets. The graves looked like beds. The new ones had polished stone 'bedspreads' that were very shiny, and the stones with the writing on were the bedheads. Often, there were big lists of names on the headstone, and I wondered where all the bodies fitted. Sometimes, there would be a whole collection of children named, with their ages carved beside the names. It was hard to imagine so many children in one family dying. I didn't know any child who had died, although I knew from books that they did do that – trees could fall on them, or they could get very sick.

The older graves were sometimes a bit split apart, and there would be a gap between the little side wall and the big stone covering the grave. The space underneath looked very black, and I would peer in nervously but never saw anything but dirt. In places,

I'd see a grave top of just dirt, our dry reddish-orange gravel, which lay there by itself with no mark or stone. I knew it was a grave because the soil was sunken like a bed whose springs had gone.

In springtime, the crunchy gravel was covered by a flat sort of soursob growing like a purple carpet around the graves. Soursobs came up in spring and made the edges of the footpaths look very pretty, but unlike these, they grew tall and yellow. Mum and Dad didn't like soursobs in the garden. They told me these were a sort of soursob too, called an oxalis. I liked their big, soft leaves and pink-purple flowers.

The cemetery was interesting to visit, but it felt quiet and lonely. I was sometimes a bit uneasy if I were by myself because I never knew who else might be there.

My friends and I could just ride out of town into the bush, and once, we stopped at a shallow creek bed to the right of the flat road. It was in the middle of nowhere with paddocks on one side and the bush on the other, with the creek bed curving through it. As usual, there was no water in it, but the bed of the creek was interesting because it was flat and covered in stones. Once we had started walking across the stones, we realised that it was a bit soggy underfoot. Then we opened our ears and heard frogs. Frogs were really exciting because we hardly ever heard them. It was usually so dry that there was never any water lying anywhere.

'Listen!'

'Where are they?'

We made such a noise that the frogs went silent.

Someone turned over a stone.

'Frog!'

There they were. It seemed that every stone had a little frog underneath it. Sometimes there were two, crouched in their wet hollow suddenly exposed to noise and light and shrill, moving towers of creatures. Their bodies were gleaming and patterned, and I loved seeing their legs jump, just like in the cartoons. We wanted to catch and hold them but the little frogs were very fast and agile, and I was afraid of hurting them if I grabbed too hard. Then we realised that although we wanted to take them home, we couldn't, because we had nothing to put them in for the long ride home. Anyway, they might die away from the creek and their stones. So, eventually we said goodbye to them and rode home. A few weeks later, out in the car with Mum on a Sunday afternoon drive, I tried to find the frog creek to show her, but couldn't.

Sometimes, if I were on a bike ride by myself and just drifted out of Eaglehawk along Sailor's Gully Road, which became a highway to somewhere, and then rode past the sign that meant that cars were allowed to go fast, the road became very quiet. I would hear my tyres thrumming on the asphalt instead of the usual crunch on gravel and the roar of cars approaching from a long way away. I didn't like them coming up from behind me and would steer onto the loose gravel between the asphalt and the little ditch by the scrub of the road reserve while they sped past. Trucks were horrible because of the noise and the wind they made. At a certain point, it would get a bit lonely, or I'd realise that I'd have to ride that same distance back again, so I would look ahead and behind before doing a swoop across the road to start riding home.

The bike gave me a very particular Eaglehawk life. On the bike, I was free to do exactly what I wanted either by myself or with a loose bunch of riding friends. These were street friends, not school friends, as I wasn't sent to the state school up the road but to a private girls' school in Bendigo, called Girton. It was too far to ride to, let alone on that huge, heavy bike.

If Jane and I didn't get a lift into school with Dad, we'd catch the tram into Bendigo. The tram stop was just up at the top of our street, opposite St Peter's Church. I could also catch it at the terminus, furthest away from home and near the park – which was nice because you always got a seat – but also at Victoria Street, Church Street and closest of all, outside our back gate through the factory and up Haggar Street.

I knew its timetable and knew that the tram's dark green snout would appear in the distance, approach and stop for me. Bendigo had two lines: the long Quarry Hill to Eaglehawk line and the shorter Golden Square to Lake Weeroona line roughly at right angles to it. They crossed at the Bendigo Fountain which took about half an hour to get to from the Eaglehawk terminus. From the Fountain, getting to school was easy, either another tram heading to Golden Square or a ten- to fifteen-minute walk. Sometimes, I'd get off at Don Street, well before Bendigo proper, and walk down the hill to Girton, neatly cutting off two sides of a triangle. I enjoyed having the choices.

Coming home by tram on a winter's afternoon, I'd sometimes stay on for an extra stop and get off at Victoria Street so I could go to Eliades' Fish and Chip Shop to buy sixpence worth of chips. It'd be warm inside the shop, and I loved watching the basket of chips plunging into the bubbling hot fat, and even better, see them spilled out crisply on to the thin white paper resting on the newspaper before being swirled into a tight little newspaper parcel. If Mr Eliades had run out of the white paper, we would sometimes find words printed on our chips. I'd hug the warmth and pick open a little hole at the top to pull the chips out. The first ones were really burny, and I'd have to blow on them as they steamed in the cold air. Usually, I'd have eaten them before I'd got home and would try to sneak the paper into the bin before going inside. Mum seemed to think that I wouldn't eat my dinner if I'd had chips beforehand. No such risk! My classmates all lived in Bendigo, so I didn't see them out of school except for the odd birthday party Mum would drive me to. One exciting school day, when I was about eight, a friend asked me to play at her house that Saturday afternoon. The mothers must have talked on the phone about it and Mum must have decided that I would go by tram, as they lived near the far end of our line. I caught the tram all the way past the Fountain and up to Quarry Hill, feeling a bit anxious about recognising the house and getting off at the right stop. I got it right and found her house, which I'd previously seen from the car.

I liked her backyard, which had a big tree in it. I thought we might build a little tree house in it, and we found some bits of wood to carry up. I went up first, carrying a little plank. It slipped out of my hand and dropped on her head. I felt awful. She went inside crying, and I climbed down and hung around outside, feeling very embarrassed and guilty. Her mother came out to bring me in and was nice about it, though. We sat in the kitchen and she gave us a drink of cordial and some biscuits. Later, we went out to play in some paddocks further up the road from her house. There was a football lying there, all by itself on the wet grass. It was old, sodden and bloated, but according to Finders Keepers, it was mine! I looked forward to taking it home so that I could have my own football to take out onto the street.

By the end of the visit, I was a bit cold in my shorts and cotton check shirt, which I'd insisted on wearing, but happy to be in a corner seat on the tram rumbling towards Eaglehawk with my new football on my lap. At the Fountain tram stop, the headmistress and the senior music teacher climbed on. They greeted me but I felt very exposed, sitting there with a soggy, smelly football on my lap. They sort of smiled to each other. How embarrassing. Luckily, they were only on for one stop and got off at the Capitol Theatre so I could go home in peace.

I don't think I had any other 'play dates' with the girls from school. Maybe that didn't happen so often in those days. Maybe children just played at home. That friend didn't come back to us to play.

When I was about eleven, a friend from school did move to Eaglehawk, and I liked that because I could just go round to her place and we would go to her room and talk. I don't think she came to our house though. I didn't have a room of my own, and somehow it didn't seem comfortable.

The tram would also take me to the pictures in Bendigo on a Saturday afternoon. Jane, Rich and I would wait at the top of Church Street, and I would have my bundle of comics with me. By the time we got into Bendigo, I was really keen to get going. We'd race up from the Fountain stop to join the queue at the Princess Theatre in View Street. If it were a good film, there'd be a queue of kids already stretching up the footpath, all talking and jiggling and moving up and down to talk to friends.

This is where the comics came in. The queue was where you swapped your comics, so I would get Jane or Rich to mind my place and would go up and down with my Superman, Phantom and Goofy comics. If I were lucky, a kid would have some that I didn't have, and I would have some that he wanted and we'd do a good swap.

Finally, the box office would open, and we'd creep forward down the street, through the glass doors, past the queue controller in his uniform, across the brightly patterned carpet towards the window and the rolls of tickets. Usually, the mother of one of our neighbourhood friends would be at work in there. She was the only mother we knew who worked. She had only one child and a husband to look after and a very neat house. I think she was a bit bored. No other mothers in the street worked – they had too many children to look after – and none of the mothers of my school friends worked.

If we had timed it right, we got to our seats, always a rush upstairs for the novelty of being up high, in time to read the comics greedily in the dim light before the programme started. We didn't usually have the money to buy anything from the ice cream and lolly lady who walked around in a uniform with a torch shining on her tray of Jaffas, Minties and dixies of ice cream.

The lights dimmed, the curtains did their opening and closing performance and the black-and-white newsreel with the laughing kookaburras started us off. Gradually, we'd quieten and settle for the B film or the group of shorts. Usually, that was pretty boring. Interval meant hanging around restlessly until we could crowd back in for the real film and beautiful big coloured pictures.

I have very few memories of what we actually saw. I loved Danny Kaye, but there were boring bits. Dean Martin and Jerry Lewis weren't bad, but the romantic bits were terrible. I must have seen some Disney films but don't remember them much. I liked the Lassie films and was terrified in the one where Lassie had to pick her way across a hillside full of striking rattlesnakes. About the most exciting memory was from a pirate film where the ship was badly holed and a crew member swam under the ship pulling a rope dragging a sail across the opening. I loved seeing the hull from the blue water underneath and the excitement of the heroic swimming. It seemed a long way from the brown waters of the Eaglehawk Baths.

The rolling credits meant a stampede to the door and a race to the tram to get a seat for the ride home.

I loved the tram because it would always come and I didn't have to wait for people to do things for me. I could decide to go into Bendigo and just take myself. The fare was threepence, and that would get me to school, the shops, the Bendigo pool and the pictures. I saw that other kids had a student's season ticket and found out how to buy one. I bought a little plastic case at Woolworths to keep it in. It felt grown-up and part of tram life to just pull the pass out and wave it at the conductor, who sometimes was the father of a friend from church.

I was lucky to be able to get around by myself and have the choice of walking, riding my bike or catching the tram. At the time, that independence and freedom seemed normal. I was able to learn my neighbourhood and develop a very clear mental map of my world. The tram and its passengers introduced me to a wider community of people of all ages going about their lives: to and from work, shopping, going to school. I became part of a life that I would never have had if I'd been driven everywhere in my parents' car.

Chapter Five
The Permeable House

I had mixed feelings about being the doctor's daughter.

On the one hand, I was proud of his brass plate screwed to the front fence with black letters spelling his name and qualifications. Mum explained that MB and BS. Melb. meant Bachelor of Medicine and Bachelor of Surgery and that Melb. meant the University of Melbourne, which is where he learnt to be a doctor. I came to realise that being the doctor was important and that a lot of people knew him and came to see him because they were sick.

On the other hand, there was a problem for me because my father was so well known locally. Many people knew who I was, but I didn't always know them: were they from the church, were they Dad's patients or did they just know who I was? I didn't know if I should look up at every face I saw in the street in case I had to say hello, or if it were safer to look at no one and run the risk of being branded snobby or rude.

One day, I got caught out up at the shops. I was walking under the deep, dusty verandahs to the newsagent to buy a comic when an old lady in a brown coat stopped me and took both my hands. *Who is she? What does she want? Why is she holding my hands?*

'Elizabeth, I just want to say that your father is a wonderful man. He saved my Ern. I don't know what I'd do without Ernie.'

She was crying by now and I was really embarrassed. It was nice to know that someone liked Dad, but I didn't know what to do. She wept and talked a bit more, said, 'Thank you, dear. God bless you!' and let me go.

I raced into Mundy's to look at the Donald Duck comics hoping no one had seen me standing there with a crying lady holding my hands.

That sort of thing happened again from time to time but usually without the weeping, and over the years, I got better at just standing there being polite and a bit proud.

As I got older, I also felt particularly conspicuous because my sister and I were sent to a private school in Bendigo. This seemed to go with being the doctor's daughters. We had to wear a boring brown uniform with hat and gloves. I hated catching the tram amongst all the high school kids in their nice navy uniforms. My brother went to the state school up the road, and I've since wondered if that was because there was no Anglican private school for boys in Bendigo. There were quite a few Catholic ones, or 'Roman' Catholic as Mum insisted, saying both religions were Catholic – a fine point!

I also became aware that we lived in a big brick house with furniture that was different from that in the smaller houses of the kids we played with. We had a 'dining room' and a 'drawing room', and there were bookshelves with Dad's books in them, a piano with Dad's music stacked on top and a gramophone with big black records of music by people called Mozart and Beethoven. We didn't have a wood stove in the kitchen like all the other houses but an electric one. However, I'd have liked a wood stove to keep us warm in winter. Mum made the house look really nice. The furniture was polished; there were vases of flowers and interesting glassy ornaments on the mantelpiece and paintings on the walls.

Unlike the other mothers I knew, Mum had a lady to come and help her with the housework. Gladys would ride her bike down the hill to us, and she and Mum would get to work cleaning the floors and the bathroom and kitchen. I liked Gladys, especially for the pastry she sometimes made for Mum, but during the school holidays when I was home, I never quite knew where to put myself and felt uncomfortable just hanging around or reading while she was working so hard for us. I should really have been given a job to do too!

Somehow, the fact that our father was the doctor – and therefore different – was complemented by the fact that he was a beautiful pianist.

Dad's piano playing rolled around our lives. He played after lunch if he had time, before dinner and later in the evening. We'd hear him playing while we were in the garden or from the street if the windows were open. Mum would report with pride that so and so had said how lovely it was to walk past and hear that beautiful music coming from the house.

We were all proud of his playing; the piano had a good sound, and he could play almost anything classical. Mozart was his favourite composer. Stacked around the piano were big heavy books of music and piles of sheet music balanced on chairs. At bedtime, my sister, brother and I lay in the dark, listening. We yelled out requests, 'Alla Turca!' and off he'd go with that exciting, rollicking tune. Mum sometimes said it was too exciting for bedtime, but we didn't think so.

My sister started piano lessons and then my brother. I'd look at their music; they'd show me the notes, and I'd play what they played until it got too hard with the sharps. I vaguely kept waiting to be told that I'd be starting to learn piano, but it never happened. I didn't ask, maybe because it seemed to be something that parents told their kids they were going to do, like going to school.

When I was much older, I asked Mum why I hadn't learnt.

'Oh, we thought you were far too much of a tomboy to want to learn!'

'Oh.'

But my brother learnt, and he was a real boy.

I would have loved to have piano lessons. I would have loved to have my Dad sitting beside me sharing his love of music and showing me what to do. You would think that seeing and hearing this little girl sitting at the piano playing her sister and brother's music and practising like them would at least make my parents think of asking her if she'd like to learn!

Most of what I knew about Dad's earlier life came from Mum chatting to me, and over the years a patchwork of stories accumulated. He never spoke about himself and, in fact, didn't talk much at all.

I learnt from Mum that after graduating and completing his residency at Launceston Hospital, which is where they met and married in 1943, the army had sent him north. He was a doctor on the hospital ships full of wounded men being brought back from New Guinea to Australia. He would get off somewhere in Queensland and then get a train back up north to pick up the next ship. She said that one ship he had worked on, Centaur, had been torpedoed by the Japanese, and many of his colleagues and friends had died. He had been on the ship on its previous voyage.

Mum said that after operating and looking after the soldiers down inside the ship, he would go up on deck for a smoke, looking at the sunset. She also told us that he hated his regulation pistol and would keep it in his drawer, whenever he could.

Dad came back from the war with TB, caught perhaps in New Britain, an island off the coast of New Guinea, where for a while he had been based as a medical officer. After the TB diagnosis, about the time Mum was pregnant with me, he was sent to the Heidelberg Repatriation Hospital (the Repat) in Melbourne for maybe about a year, getting quite plump, according to a couple of family photos, and weaving the blankets and scarves, sewing the leather purses and satchels and assembling the cut-out felt pictures which became part of our family possessions. I was born during this time. When he was well again, he worked as a resident doctor at the Bendigo Base Hospital for about another year and must have occasionally stayed at the bank with us.

I found out more about Dad in our woodshed. The door was usually open, but one day I closed it for some reason and something strange bulked up in front of me. Hanging from a nail was a wool army jacket, heavy and covered in dust and cobwebs. Underneath the jacket was a light canvas shoulder bag. I was uneasy looking at these things there in the woodshed and was afraid of being caught. It felt like a sort of secret because Dad never spoke about being in the army, but here was the physical evidence that he actually had been a soldier. He seemed so unlike a fighting man that it was hard to understand how he did it. I couldn't even imagine him marching in step. If he didn't want to talk about it, why were the clothes there, neither thrown out in the rubbish nor in the house in a wardrobe? I showed them to my sister and brother, and we stood there puzzled and scared of being found looking. It seemed private.

Over the years, these disturbingly out-of-place clothes stayed hidden. From time to time, I would look to see if they were still there. It always felt uncomfortable as the dark, heavy, not quite abandoned army tunic had a confused and frightening atmosphere about it.

It wasn't only the jacket that made the woodshed an ambiguous place. One Saturday afternoon, it became an informal operating theatre. Smokey, our elegant grey cat, which Dad had brought home from a litter found in the hospital's tunnels, needed an operation to remove his little furry balls before he could make female cats have kittens no one would want. I remembered that Ginger, our first cat, had gone to the vet to have that operation, but this time, Dad thought that he would be able to do it. So he cleared a space on the bench, brought out the bottle of ether and some instruments and went to find Smokey.

We were swarming around wanting to watch, but Dad shooed us out before he put some ether on a pad to make Smokey go to sleep. We kids stood nervous and giggling about halfway between the shed and the kitchen, where Mum was busy radiating disapproval. Suddenly, Smokey dashed out through the connected garage, streaking down the drive and trailing stainless steel instruments. He'd woken, scratched Dad and escaped. We didn't like this. Poor Smokey! Jane cried, Rich and I were jumping up and down and yelling, and Mum brought us inside. Dad found Smokey and finished the operation. Mum told us that at least Smokey wouldn't have been frightened by going to the vet! A sleepy Smokey was brought into the house to recover, woke and lived a long and, I hope, happy and kittenless life. Our next cat, Chloe, went to the vet!

Our house often felt too confused and busy. It always seemed to have patients in it, about to be in it or ringing up wanting Dad. Those of his patients who had cars would park them out the front on the road and sometimes outside Wowo and Wally's place. The patients would walk up our front path, up the verandah's central steps, cross the verandah and step into the waiting room, which was really the first bit of our central hall partitioned off at the archway. We had a large chest of drawers placed against the partition on our family side.

On the waiting room side was a table for magazines. The patients sat on two rows of chairs against the hall walls and waited to go into the surgery, which was the front room on the left. Mum and Dad's bedroom was on the front right and a door opened from it into the waiting room. Sometimes, a new patient would open that door by mistake and be terribly embarrassed to see a bedroom, sometimes with Mum or us in it. Another door opened from Mum and Dad's room into our bedroom, which they had to go through to get to and from the hall and the rest of the house. I was always aware of the presence of people just behind the chest of drawers. We could hear them chatting and they would certainly have heard us kids during the school holidays. Sometimes, Dad would come through telling us to be quiet.

The patients rang the doorbell before entering, and that sound rang through to a bell at the back of the house where we'd be. The phone would ring, and no one would want to answer it because it would nearly always be for Dad. It was really hard to answer the phone when Mum and Dad weren't around and have to respond to someone whose wife had 'had a turn'. The caller would not have wanted to talk to me either. I learnt to take messages but to avoid the phone if at all possible. The phone would ring in the night, and sometimes the front doorbell would ring at night, and I would hear Dad talking to the person and then hear the car going down the drive. He would never complain about going on a call.

Sometimes, a patient would knock at the back door when no one had come to the front door. If Mum and Dad didn't answer, I'd go and open the door.

'Is your Dad in, love?'

He might have been in the garden, or if it were a Saturday, he might have been up at the church practising his organ music for the service next day. Mum also might have been up at the church doing the flowers. I would know what to say but felt shy and inadequate and resentful. I quite liked sending the patient up to the church to find Dad and interrupt him.

In the evenings, after dinner, he would go into the drawing room by himself to smoke and read his medical journals. There was a stack of them on the coffee table, and they were too hard for me to read, though I tried. Mum would tell us not to interrupt him. The journal reading seemed to be very important and revered. Mum said that it was important for him to read them so that he would be up to date with his medical knowledge.

As an adult, I learnt, via Mum of course, that he was regarded by the nursing staff at the Base Hospital as a very good diagnostician and geriatric doctor. It helped to know that he was good at the job he worked so hard at.

I felt proud when a patient came to the back door to thank Dad with gifts. Sometimes, this was because they hadn't been able to pay his fee. He was brought big fresh lettuces and freshly shot ducks and rabbits. One of his patients liked to knit him socks, and they were beautiful to look at, with the fancy lines of stitches at the heel. Dad liked wearing them.

In addition to the house being full of patients, Dad's father, Pa, started to live with us for months at a time. Mum said that he couldn't live by himself any more because he was old. He would stay at his other son's house for a few months, then come and live with us and then go to his daughter's house. I was about six when this started, and Mum said that I had met him once while we were on holiday at Dromana.

This first time, the whole family went to meet him at the Bendigo Station. It was dark and cold and the platform was crowded with people waiting to pick up relatives and friends who were coming up from Melbourne. The enormous black steam engine rushed into the platform, its whistle screaming, its headlight blinding us, snorting steam from its sides and funnel, and roaring louder than anything I had ever heard. The wheels were huge; the pistons plunged back and forth; the train driver was high above us and the platform filled with steam. Two-year-old Richie was terrified and cried loudly. He had to be picked up, and we had to find Pa. I didn't remember what he looked like. The steam cleared and Dad walked towards a small crumpled man in a suit standing by a suitcase. Above Richie's crying, Mum said, 'That's Pa.'

Pa slept in the back bedroom, which Mum had made nice for him. At dinner time, he would sit next to Dad, and I would come into the kitchen to see him already sitting at the table while Mum was mashing the potatoes or doing other jobs finishing off the dinner. One day, I noticed that when his meal was dished up and put in front of him, he would touch the rim of the plate with his right index finger. Then I noticed that Dad did just the same.

'Why do Dad and Pa touch their plates before they eat?' I asked Mum later when I was drying the dishes.

She sighed and slumped at the sink.

'They're checking to see if the plate's been warmed before I dished up.'

'Oh.'

I didn't really understand that but didn't like that it upset Mum.

I knew she had to work very hard with washing and ironing and shopping and cooking and cleaning to look after us, plus answering the phone.

In winter, I'd come home from school and go to the 'Warm Ray' wood stove in the dining room to warm up. It was good to stand in front of it and feel the heat on my cold bare legs. Pa would be sitting in the chair angled towards the fire and be pleased to see me. He'd ask what I'd learnt in school that day, which I'd tell him. He had been a primary school headmaster, so we could have a good talk. Then he'd start quizzing me on times tables, spelling and general knowledge. I loved those moments when I'd stand in front of the fire and answer his questions really quickly and well. We both enjoyed it.

As the years went by, the quizzing game became not so interesting and slower. I complained about it one day to Mum, and she said, 'Oh, Lizzie, you've got older and you've got past what he knows. He's got older too so he's not as fast.'

He got even older and deafer and withdrawn. I was sorry to have that contact fade, and as that friendly interaction ceased, Pa became just someone else filling up the house and the kitchen table and making work for Mum. He became ill, which made it even harder for Mum to look after him and us.

I didn't like all of this co-habitation. I felt uneasy and nervous about all the bells ringing, about strangers being so intimately in our house but so distantly – as if they were there but not there. I never knew who was going to appear, where, or when, or what they'd want. The permeability of my house made me feel exposed.

These days, I live with my husband, Nick, in a flat, up high and separated from the street and people by security doors. I love it. I don't hear cars pulling up, I can wear exactly what I want;

I'm not on show and I feel quiet and safe. I ring friends, they ring me, and I can be as sociable as I like on my terms. I know that some people like a neighbourly 'drop-in any time' sort of sociability, and in fact, I appreciated that when I was home with small children, but not now. I relish the times when I am quietly alone in our flat and can just be.

It was complicated being the 'doctor's daughter'. However, all the playing with the kids in our street gave me a sort of immunity from being seen as stuck-up. In fact, I only remember one occasion when being the doctor's daughter was held against me. I had been out on my bike playing down near the park when one of the kids said, 'Come to our place. We've got a really good tree.' We whizzed into their dirt drive, beside their house, which seemed to be trying to subside into the ground, dumped our bikes amongst all the old toys lying around and swarmed up the huge pepper tree, yelling to each other like a flock of cockatoos. We were still there when their dad walked up the drive, looked up at us and yelled to his wife, 'Who's that up there?' looking at me.

She came out the back door, stared up into the tree and said, 'Oh, that's the doctor's daughter.'

He yelled, 'Get 'er out of 'ere. We don't want the likes of 'er around,' and lurched through his back door.

The mother called up, 'You'd better go home, love.'

I climbed down fast, said, 'Thanks for having me,' and rode off. I was afraid of that man.

I always felt a bit uneasy with Dad, especially when it was just him and me in a room. Perhaps this was because of the lack of early contact, and it wasn't helped that, by nature, he was not an open, kind, loving man. He would lose his temper quickly and unpredictably. Possibly, this was explained by his war experiences, the stress of setting up his own practice and having three young children in the household, but this adult insight was of no help to me at the time.

I would have loved to have had an open, friendly relationship with him and really liked it when men were friendly and cheerful with me, like the locum we had one year for our summer holiday. Mum had been working hard to get the house nice for him and his family. When they arrived and we weren't ready, I decided that I would tie down the suitcases which were to go on the roof rack. I was on the roof of the car sorting out the cases and rope when the doctor, who was rather handsome, came out the back door and said, 'Do you want a hand?' He had a smile in his voice. I replied, 'I'm alright, thanks,' and went on tying down the luggage. He came up to the car.

'I do know my knots, you know. I was in the navy.'

I looked up at his eyes, grinned, said, 'Alright' and jumped off the roof. He had the cases tied down in a flash, and, indeed, his knots were very neat.

I still feel happy thinking about this exchange.

Neither was Dad easy to have as a public figure of a father because he wasn't a blokey sort of man. His shyness made him an awkward conversationalist, and he could sometimes seem rude and abrupt. Maybe I was more self-conscious of this than I needed to be.

On the other hand, he was an educated, cultured man and gave us the gift of filling the house with music and books. The books were there to take or leave. I took the offer and read whatever I could, including comics.

Eaglehawk Girl

I had discovered comics at Mundy's Newsagent up in the main street. They'd be spread out in stands along with *The Women's Weekly* and *The Woman's Day* and the other magazines. They had coloured covers, and the Disney ones even had coloured pictures inside. Mr Mundy would get cross and tell us kids off if we tried to sneak a read without buying. I had enough pocket money to buy a comic occasionally. The Disney ones were my first buys, and I enjoyed the silliness and ease of Donald Duck and Goofy.

I liked building up a stack of comics and started adding Superman. I enjoyed the story of his birth and the planet and kryptonite and Clark Kent and the phone box transformations. Lois Lane was a bit of a nuisance. Superman's costume was fun and I loved the illustrations of him flying. I was interested in the way he thrust out one arm and sort of raised one leg. It was a bit hard to imagine how you would arrange your body if you were flying, and I decided that there would be a difference between just floating in the sky when you'd probably just do a sort of breaststroke and the speeding type of flying when you would want to be sort of pointy, like Superman. It'd be fun to have a cloak to blow out behind you.

I'd buy Batman but never liked him as much as Superman. I didn't like the city setting or the other characters or the car. It all seemed crowded and the pictures were very dense and black.

My preference for the outdoors was happily satisfied with the Phantom, 'The Ghost who Walks'. He lived in Africa in a cave and had adventures whilst 'doing good'.

I didn't realise this as a child, but the goal of all these heroes was to fight evil and seek justice. There was a sense of right and wrong and justice. I think I was developing a strong sense of fairness and these heroes consolidated it. It's interesting to think about this in conjunction with the message, which upset me, from Tootle and

Scuffy about conformity and the crushing of dreams.

My comic stack got bigger and bigger, and I loved sorting through them and having a reread. Mum and Dad didn't like them much, especially Dad, and I realised that I needed to hide them from him. I found what I thought was a good place in our old outside dunny. Eaglehawk had just had the sewerage put on and we didn't need the old pan in the outhouse any more, so I put my stack of comics on the wooden bench, next to the central cut out hole and its wooden lid. I knew other people used to have a stack of magazines in their dunnies, and I would go and sit there, reading my comics secretly and peacefully.

The secret didn't last long. I was in the kitchen one day with Mum when Dad came into the house waving my bundle of comics above his head. He was furious.

'Have you still got these awful things! I'm going to burn them!'

'No!' I jumped up and down in front of him. 'They're mine.'

He went out the back door. 'I'm going to burn them. They're rubbish.'

I ran out after him, jumping around but not game enough to get close and snatch them off him. By now, I was between him and the incinerator, but he kept on walking, waving my comics in the air.

'No. They're mine. It's my pocket money. I can spend my pocket money on what I want.'

'American rubbish!'

'I read other things. I read books. I read English books. I've read *Alice in Wonderland*. I've read *Peter Pan and Wendy* and *Wind in the Willows* and all the Enid Blyton books and Gulliver's Travels, and I know about David Copperfield. I've read all the books at school. I go to the library. It's not fair!'

He deflated, threw the comics on the ground and walked away.

I was scared but gathered them up, straightened their front

covers and hugged them. I nearly had a cry to myself out there on the back lawn but had to think about what to do. I decided to hide them in my cubby house where Dad would be too big to get in the door. I did keep on buying comics but very secretly.

There was a big problem with punctuality in our family, which was often related to Dad and his work. For a long time, Jane and I had trouble getting to school in Bendigo on time. Some days of the week, we'd get a ride with Dad, who'd be going to the Bendigo Base Hospital to do his rounds. We'd pile into the back seat, me behind the driver's side, in uniforms and hats with our bags on our laps. And we'd wait. Dad would eventually emerge, and off we'd go, backing down the drive, up Church Street, left onto the main road, over Job's Gully Bridge and through Cal Gully, then Long Gully and down Don Street to be dropped at the front gates of junior school.

If Dad hadn't left it too late, the girls would still be playing in the yard, waiting for Miss Cure to ring the bell for us to line up neatly for prayers in the hall. But if Dad had dawdled more than usual, there'd be an empty yard. If it wasn't too late, the girls would still be lined up waiting and we could race in, dump our bags under Miss Cure's disapproving eye and join our place in the line. It was worse if the yard was empty and worst of all if the singing had started. That meant we had to go to a back door and enter the hall, trying to be silent and invisible but knowing that all the teachers would see us as we crept in, late yet again, to stand in the row of late girls. We would lose or earn mysterious points for all this lateness and eventually would have to 'stay in' and write out lines about lateness.

Eventually, I realised that I could relieve a lot of that morning anxiety by catching the tram to school every day. It was comforting to get to school in time to play in the yard before prayers. However, it meant being up at the tram stop by ten past eight, which was easy in summer but not so good on cold winter mornings, when I'd have to crunch across the frost on the back lawn. The car ride beckoned then, even with the 'late' risk. Choices, again!

I learnt very much later, from Mum, that Dad's hospital rounds started well after school started and that he didn't like hanging around waiting in the car park at the hospital. The outcome of that dilemma was that either we were late or he was early!

This waiting also happened at evening events at school, when the whole family would be sitting in the car waiting for him to come out the back door and get in the car before we could leave. Once, I had to be snuck on to the stage, after having raced around the back of the hall in dark to the stage door. The concert had started, the teachers were cross and it was awful. I hated being ready but waiting and waiting to be taken places.

Sometimes, the occasional picking-up arrangements went wrong. It was a treat to be picked up by Mum after school if she'd been doing something in Bendigo in the afternoon, like her lampshade-making class at the School of Mines. I loved rushing out the gates to see the car nosed into the footpath waiting for us, but there were days when she was a bit late.

For a long time, we just had the one car. It was a 'bathtub' Vanguard. That upside-down-bathtub car was so embarrassing, especially as my surname, Trembath, already had *bath* in it. I used to be taunted with, 'Trem trembles in the bath!' Later, there was a far less conspicuous grey Vanguard which had squarish corners. Dad had first priority on the car to call on patients, and this caused a lot of problems. Mum would arrive late, calling out the window, 'I had to wait for the car,' and we'd grumble and climb in, usually pretty relieved.

Not always!

One afternoon, my sister and I stood waiting outside the gates. Off went Diane, our last friend there. I watched enviously as she drove away with her mother. Now, there were no big girls waiting at the bottom senior school gate, and we were the last little girls left at the top gate. The classrooms and most of the yard were behind the crumbling yellow wall we leant against. Anyway, we weren't allowed to play on the swings or see-saw after school, and if we did, we might miss seeing the car coming down the hill.

I walked around, kicking the stones in the wall's foundations on each circuit. I stood on the locked gate's bottom rail jiggling it as I looked into the empty asphalt yard. The chalked dodgie court was still marked out. At lunchtime, the yard had been full of girls screaming as they dodged the ball and the swings were swooping high and the see-saws thumping. Now the magpies patrolled the grounds picking up the lunch scraps that the yard monitors had pretended not to see.

Miss Cure hadn't left yet. I ran down to the other gate to see what was happening. The boarders had stopped playing sport and the bottom yard was empty too. It was getting quieter, and each approaching car could be heard. We stepped out onto the road to look, but each time, it wasn't ours.

I heard Miss Cure's footsteps crossing the yard to the gate. We stood together, backs to the wall, near our brown leather satchels. The little gate rattled and she appeared.

'Oh! You girls are still here!'

'Yes, Miss Cure.'

'Are you being picked up?'

'Yes. Mum probably had to wait for the car.'

'Well, then.' And over the road she went to her gloomy weatherboard house diagonally opposite the school. We watched her open her gate and go in.

We played a game of hoppie.

A siren blared. It was knock-off time at Milne's, the metalwork factory over the road. Men walked out the big roller door, slinging bags over their shoulders and shouting to their mates as they got into their cars or walked down to the tram stop. The surge became a trickle as the last office workers left. A huge clatter rang out as the roller door was lowered and locked by a man in a suit. Only a couple of cars were parked under the elms now. The street was quiet and empty. The man stretched, looked over the road and saw two small girls in brown uniforms and berets standing by their bags. He paused, then came over to us.

'Are you waiting for your mum?'

'Yes.'

'It's a bit late, isn't it?'

'Yes. She has to wait for the car.'

He paused, 'Oh, well. Good luck!'

He turned back across the road and drove off.

Now there were no people anywhere.

Was it getting dark?

Was that the car? No.

I saw movement across the road. Miss Cure came out of her gate across to us. I stood up tall as she approached. I was ashamed of being left on the street for so long. Miss Cure didn't seem to know what to do. She waited an embarrassing few minutes with us before clicking back across the road in her solid heels.

Finally, the two-tone grey Vanguard rolled down the road and pulled over outside Milne's. We ran across. I couldn't speak. I was trying not to cry.

I'm now the sort of adult who is always just a bit early, the sort of person who frets a bit if kept waiting to meet someone. I fuss about whether I'm in the right place at the right time. I like my arrangements to be really clear and other people to be on time. I love arriving to meet a friend and find that she is already there, waiting for me! It's a sort of reverse waiting anxiety but much better than out-of-control rushing and powerlessness.

The garden was less complicated than the house. The patch of concrete out the back door was where I first started playing outside by myself. It was a good-sized square, warmed by the morning sun and bordered on two sides by the back room and the laundry. Mum put toys out there for us to play with. We had a little table and chairs which I'd ride my trike round and round while my sister played with dolls and tea sets.

If I got sick of circling my sister, I could pedal across the back lawn to the swing. Two thick round posts supported a cross-beam which had a couple of thin ropes tied to it, making a swing for very young children. Even after I grew out of it, I liked sitting there gently rocking and looking at the almond tree, which gave afternoon shade in summer. In spring, the tree was covered with pink blossom, and I loved looking at the blue sky through the pink flowers and the tiny bits of green leaves. However, spring brought a bee hazard. Dad had planted Easter daisies against the posts, and each year, they grew taller and taller and attracted more and more bees. It was a bit scary brushing past bee-laden flowers. The lawn had soft dark green grass, and in summer, we played with the hose and sprinkler, squirting each other and screaming around in our wet undies.

Round the side was an old mulberry tree. It was subsiding towards the fence, and the sloping thick trunk was easy to climb and sit on. We could scramble out onto the branches which forked to each side and sit up there amongst the foliage. It was a perfect first climbing tree, and the kids from next door would come in to climb with us. The amazing thing was that this tree produced fruit without any blossom that we could see. Each year, one day, out of nowhere, I'd notice small, hard, nubbly green mulberries amongst the leathery leaves. They took ages to ripen and I'd test a red one and spit it out – so sour! When they were nearly black and starting to fall, we'd sit in the tree and eat and eat. Purple mouths, purple teeth, purple clothes.

I knew that silk worms ate mulberry leaves and that Les, the big teenage boy who lived in the house diagonally behind us, kept silk worms. Mum used to give his mother mulberry leaves for him. I took some in one day and he offered to show me the silk worms. He had a box full of scruffy half-eaten leaves and a few small white caterpillars. It didn't look very interesting, but I was puzzled by all the little black specks on the bottom.

'What are those black things?' I asked.

'Oh,' said Les, looking a bit red and hesitant, 'that's their poo.'

'Oh.'

He showed me a tiny little sort of prickly wheel with a handle and said that he wound the silk around it to turn it into thread. I couldn't understand how that worked but was too shy by now to ask another question.

The mulberries were delicious compared to the cherry plums which grew in a thicket against the nearby fence. The cherry plum branches had thorns, beautiful white blossom and really sour fruit which went from green to red through every shade in between. You were lucky to find one that tasted sweet and nice.

Mum used to stew cherry plums for dessert. I was not very keen on cherry plums and custard but ate them, to the accompaniment of Mum and Dad saying things like, 'Delicious.' There was not much flesh on a cherry plum and a lot of pip. Our bowls would end up with a semi-circle of cherry plum pips balanced on the lip. We'd count them to see who had endured the most sourness.

Still in the side garden, but where it started to become the front garden, were the fish pond and the statue. A door from the drawing room opened onto the side verandah, and between it and the fence was a round pond whose concrete rim was decorated with white quartz rocks. It was about two yards in diameter and had a central column, upon which stood a tall white statue of a lady with a sort of sheet draped around most of her. Goldfish swam beneath the water lily pads.

Later, the lady got moved to stand in the garden near the fence, leaving the column in the centre of the pond as an invitation to climb up on. I wanted to stand on top of the column like the statue. I stood on the rim of the pond and leant towards the column until I had to let myself go and fall towards it. My hands caught it and there I was, like a bridge. *Hmm. What now!* I thought, and tried to grab a foothold on the column with one foot but couldn't reach that far. It was a bit tricky getting back from being a bridge. I had to push really hard with my hands and arms and rock back to step on to the ground. I'd keep trying from different positions around the rim and, when I was a bit bigger, managed to get two hands and two feet on the column, but I could never get myself up to stand right on the top.

The front verandah was good to play on when it rained, but we weren't allowed to while Dad had surgery because we'd have been right in front of his window. Otherwise, it was good for trike riding: up and down, up and down.

Overall, there was something prickly about the front garden. The grass on the rectangular lawn was grey-green with tough leaves and was called Buffalo grass because it was very tough. It was also thick and bouncy and good to play 'hoppo bumpo' on because it didn't hurt much when you fell. In hoppo bumpo, which we usually played in teams, you had to hop around with your arms crossed and bump into opponents to make them fall over. Sometimes, we'd play without teams and just surge around knocking over anyone in sight till there was just one of us left standing. British Bulldog also had a lot of rushing, grabbing, knocking down and wrestling on the grass.

On summer evenings, the front lawn was often full of kids because they would hear or sense a game was happening and just appear. We'd play until dark.

If there weren't a lot of us, we'd migrate from the lawn to the front hedge, which consisted of tough, bushy and sticky cypress. It was about three to four feet high and strong enough to support a lying-down body. It was good fun to crawl across it trying not to fall through, and sometimes I stood up and managed a little run. Again, we'd shout and make a racket and only come in when it became too dark to see. I'd be scratched, itchy and hot. A bath didn't seem to do much good with the itchy scratches, and it was a better winter game when we had more clothes on. We were pushing Mum's and Dad's patience with this game because we knew that we could easily break the hedge and make it look scruffy.

The drive running along the other side of the house was long and straight, but we mostly played up at the garage end where it widened out into a sort of turning circle.

Because the gravel was fine, we could draw circles for marbles games. I had a collection of marbles that I was very proud of: cat's eyes in all colours, stony agates and tom bowlers, which I used for the 'dropping-on-marbles-from-above' game. I kept them in a little drawstring cloth bag which Mum had made for me. By the time it had worn through, I was able to use the sewing machine myself and made a new one.

In the middle of a game one day, I was astonished to be accused of fernudging! What was that?

'You cheated! You fernudged!'

'What's *fernudge*?'

The boy from over the road showed what I'd done. I'd pushed my hand forward a bit before flicking out the marble. It gave me about a whole inch of advantage. We were all deeply into fernudging awareness after that. It was a word that stayed with marbles and didn't appear in other games.

In the hopscotch season, we drew hoppie grids. In the skipping season, we skipped. In the cricket season, we played French cricket, which Mum showed us because she knew it from when she was a little girl. All year round, I hit tennis balls against the laundry wall or played throwing and chanting games against it with a tennis ball.

We all learnt to drive on our driveway. From when I was big enough to see over the bonnet, I would sit in the driver's seat and imagine changing the gears and doing that thing with the clutch. Then I started taking the car keys from the top of the fridge and would go out and start the engine. For a while, I was happy to sit there and feel the engine running. Next, I asked Mum how it all worked; she'd explain and I'd practise. I'd go up and down by myself getting the gear changes smooth and becoming really good at reversing. The drive was long enough to get up to third gear by the kitchen window, but I'd have to brake hard to stop in front of the garage doors. I remember Richie roaring past the kitchen window, and I think even Mum was a bit startled by that. I'm amazed they let us do this.

The driveway was a bit like a public thoroughfare. Each day, the first person up it was the milkie, whose horse would quietly and steadily crunch down the road pulling his load of bottled milk from Sandhurst Dairies. The milkie ran from side to side, grabbing bottles from the cart and delivering milk to each house, in the dark in winter and in the very early light in summer. We all thought he must be very fit to do all that running. If I were awake early, I'd hear the milk bottles rattling as he brought them up our drive, and then I'd hear the plonk as he put them down on the corner of the verandah.

The baker was the next in the day. He had a van. If we were home on holidays, we would be very keen for him to arrive at the backdoor with the basket of warm, fragrant bread on his arm and even some buns, yeast buns, all fruity with a sticky black top, or a large round Boston bun with coconut icing. We would hang around Mum, looking and pestering for buns. Sometimes, we'd get one.

The groceries would be delivered to the kitchen table after Mum had bought them up at Halls, and sometimes at the end of the day, the butcher would drop in some meat on his way home to his house further up the street.

Then there'd be the dunny pan man. The sewage wasn't put on till I was about ten, and like all Eaglehawk houses, we had a dunny in the backyard. When I was little, I always felt I had to be a bit careful with how I sat and balanced over the hole above the pan. We would be pleased to have a new pan to replace the rather full one, but did not want to coincide with its delivery. I had a horror, shared with the whole family, of sitting on the dunny, hearing the man's footsteps coming up the drive, having the flap door opened, the full pan slid out and the empty one slid in – all under my bare bottom. His truck was low and heavily stacked with pans and growled slowly up the street. I felt sorry for the pan man because his job would be awful and his nose would be full of stink all day.

We'd sometimes see the Watkins man coming past the kitchen window towards the back door trying to sell cleaning products which Mum usually bought at the grocer or chemist. Mum would feel sorry for him, and we'd hide in the kitchen wishing she wouldn't buy things which would always smell odd and not quite work as they were meant to. In hindsight, I'm glad she bought from him, as he was earning a living doing this, but I just hated the general uncomfortable feeling of him trying to sell us something we didn't really want.

In our early days at Eaglehawk, there seemed to be an informal right of way through our garden to our back gate leading to the block with the big empty hall and into the next street. I could be looking out the kitchen window and see a stranger heading up the drive and towards the back path and the back gate. It was worse if I was in the garden and met her face to face. That was embarrassing for both of us. Gradually, this stopped, perhaps as we inhabited the garden more.

The white weatherboard garage and shed stood at the top of the drive. The car mostly sat outside the garage as it was easier for Dad to come and go, so we were able to play inside. The woodshed was divided off by a three-quarter-high timber wall which we could climb up on and did, just because we could.

Apart from firewood, the lawn mower and garden tools in the shed, there was a bench covered in dusty tins and tools (Smokey's operating table). I learnt to use the hammer and saw and got used to buying the nails I needed from Fitzpatrick's Hardware Shop up the street. They got weighed and given to me in a little paper bag. I also bought skipping ropes at Fitzpatrick's.

It often seemed a bit touch and go whether we'd run out of wood for the Warm Ray before Mr Clymo delivered a new load. I'd be at school when this happened, but Rich would be home for lunch from the state school when he'd hear Mr Clymo give orders to his huge horse, and he would run to watch from the house windows as this horse with big hairy feet backed the cart full of firewood up the narrow drive. The high cart wheels crunched on the gravel and the horse made loud harrumphing noises as it pushed its load up to the top of the drive. After Mr Clymo unloaded the wood, he'd climb back onto his cart and chirrup at the horse, which then trotted calmly back to the road. I'd have loved to have seen that.

However, it was good to come home from school and see a pile of logs dumped in front of the shed. Hooray, no more skimping. It pleased Mum when we kids stacked it, so we'd work hard to get it into the shed neatly up against the back wall. I thought of the idea of having the big wood one end and the small wood the other so that we'd easily be able to pick out the size we needed to carry inside or chop.

I used to chop a lot of the firewood because I felt sorry for Mum having to do it herself. I'd seen her in her apron looking really tired and chopping wood for the fire in the near dark and trying to get dinner ready for us at the same time. Dad didn't seem to think that it was his job to chop the firewood and bring it in, like Wally did for Wowo. So I thought I would learn to do it to help Mum and look after her. I enjoyed getting the knack of how to make the logs split cleanly by looking at the top to avoid the telltale wriggly, curly grain which would mean that the axe would just bounce off and not get into the wood

We only lit the fire in the afternoon even if it was a freezing frosty morning. Mum was a good fire setter and explained that the fire got going well if you went from kindling to small to middle to big wood. After that, you could put on a big un-split log, which burnt for longer. I would cut a pile of kindling, a pile of little wood, one of medium wood and one of big split pieces. She told me, as a secret, that Dad always made a smoky struggling fire because he wouldn't use middle wood. I loved setting a pyramid of kindling on top of the crumpled newspaper in the speckly cream Warm Ray, lighting it in a couple of places, closing the door and watching through the murky door panels as the yellow and orange flames roared into life.

Dad was the one who did the gardening. You knew that if the car was at home and if he wasn't in the surgery, nor in the drawing room playing the piano, he'd be somewhere in the garden. He had a great capacity for somehow drifting away sideways through an open door while we thought we were having a conversation with him, and this drift often took him all the way to the garden.

One day, he dug a hole in the lawn near the front gate and had a small tree in a pot sitting on the ground beside it. I went over to watch him put the tree in the hole and fill the hole with dirt. I was interested to see a miniature tree and looked at the tiny branches, planning in my mind to put a big swing on one of them. I pointed to one I liked the look of.

'Can I have a swing on that when the tree grows?' I asked.

'It won't be as big as that,' Dad replied, 'and it'll grow too slowly. You'll be grown-up before it.'

I was disappointed. It seemed a long time to wait. It was a bit hard to understand that there were some things that I was now too big for, like being swung around like a whizzy aeroplane by my uncle, and some things that I was far too little for.

However, what did grow more quickly were soft little plants called seedlings, which Dad brought home wrapped up in damp newspaper. He'd plant them in front of the verandah, and we would be allowed to water them. Once, he asked us to get some manure left by the delivery horses out on the road. He said that he'd pay threepence for two buckets. I ran out and filled up a couple of buckets and brought them to him and was very pleased with my money. Another time, I wanted some lollies but had no money and remembered the manure. I went and filled a couple of buckets and brought them to him in the side garden.

'Here's some manure for you. Can I have threepence, please?'

'I didn't ask for those!' He turned away and kept on digging.

Oh! I didn't understand why he wanted something one day and not another. I was left standing there with two buckets of manure and feeling let down and angry.

I was a bigger kid when he was preparing to plant a lemon bush in the back garden. This time, he dug a big hole and put some manure (not provided by me) in the bottom. The lemon was a Meyer lemon. I was hovering around when I realised that, when I had been flipping through the magazines in the dining room looking for something to read, there was an article about lemons in the *Your Garden* magazine. I raced inside and read the article very carefully, went back to Dad and started telling him all that I'd read about preparation of the soil, watering in and long-term care of the lemon tree. Dad kept on working while I was spouting all this information, then stood up, stretched his back and said, 'Oh, yes,' and walked off to the shed for something. Again, I was left standing there feeling a bit silly.

I went on reading the gardening magazine from time to time. I liked seeing the photographs of plants and learning their names. The love of plants and gardens is still with me, and now, in our flat, I do miss stepping out the door to a garden.

Over the years, Dad planted a lot of fruit trees around the side and back fences. We had plums, apples, quinces, pears, apricots and figs. Years later, in summer, I could ride down the drive, stop by the apricot tree and pick a warm, freckled apricot to eat as I rode off.

Down at the park one day, I saw that the tall green plants with big leaves and bright flowers called cannas had seed pods starting to peel open, revealing rows of shiny black seeds. I gathered a pocket full of them and rode home with a plan.

'Will these grow if I plant them?' I asked Mum, holding out a handful of beautiful smooth, gleaming seeds.

'What are they?'

'They're cannas. From the park.'

'You could try them, I suppose?'

'Where?'

'Um, by the back fence might be alright.'

She was getting lunch ready and not very interested, but I went and got the spade from the shed and had a look at the back fence. Yes, I could fit a row behind the fruit trees, and the hose would reach that far so I'd be able to water them. I dug a lot of little holes in a row and sprinkled seeds into each one and covered them up with the soil. Then I dragged the hose up there and watered them all in.

I kept watering them and soon, there were little green shoots in clumps along the row. They were growing! They kept on growing until they were really tall, and then they started flowering with twisty dark and light orange blooms and a few red ones, which I liked the best. I was so pleased with that row of tall flowering plants.

The garden was where photographs were taken. Mum had a box camera which had a yellow film inside it. The camera came out on special occasions where we were lined up for a photo. Usually, it was a Sunday and we were in our good clothes.

I came to realise that I did not want to stand like a good girl for a photo. For photos, I would generally refuse to sit nicely and would splay out my legs. Amazingly, Mum put up with that!

I liked to make the picture interesting and look as if I were doing something. Aged about five, I got Mum to wait while I moved the ladder to under the pear tree so I could stand up on it looking as if I were picking pears. At a picnic near Big Hill, I arranged the three of us on a big granite boulder. At the beach, I froze us in running poses down the sand dunes.

One Sunday, Mum had us all lined up ready for a photo in the back garden when I suddenly thought of wattle hats. 'Wait. Wattle hats!'

We ran into the back block where the Cootamundra tree was in full golden flower, chose big puffy clumps to put on our heads and posed like that.

One spring, I brought some frog spawn home from a pond near the lake and made a home for it in an old baking dish which Mum had given me. It had gravel on the bottom, some floating grass and a nice sloping rock in the middle. The black eggs got wriggly and became tadpoles. The tadpoles became huge and grew back legs. Some even had tiny front legs and would crawl out onto the rock, where I'd see their sides panting as they learnt to breathe. Each day, I checked the water level so that they could easily climb up the slanting rock.

I'd placed the baking dish amongst some plants in the garden outside the back door where they were nice and sheltered, and each day when I came home from school, I'd go and check their froggy progress. One day, I stopped to look on the way to the back door and there was no baking dish.

'What!' I yelled. 'Where are they?'

I raced inside to the kitchen.

'Where are my tadpoles?' I asked Mum.

'Oh, darling. Pa tipped them out.' She wiped her hands on her apron.

'What! They're my tadpoles. They were nearly frogs!'

'Yes. He said that he thought it was just an old dish full of dirty water. He was doing some gardening and tidied it up.'

I went out to see if there were any tadpole bodies in the grass but there weren't. It was hard to believe that Pa really didn't know what he was doing, especially as Mum didn't seem to believe him either. Gradually, I got over my tadpole sadness and became friends with him again.

I only have a flicker of memory of the fire under the copper in the outdoor laundry and mum stirring the cauldron of clothes with a stick. Jane and Richie were in their pushers parked in the warmth, and I'd be roaming around. She had to lift the clothes from the copper to the first concrete trough full of rinsing water, then turn the handle on a wringer to transfer them to the second trough, which was full of blue water from the little cloth parcel of Reckitt's Blue. She liked the blue because she said that it made the white clothes and sheets look whiter. She'd swivel the wringer around and wind the blue-rinsed clothes into the wicker laundry basket on the floor.

Then we'd all go up to the clothes line up at the back of the garden, past the little swing and near the back fence. Long wires were strung between two short boards that swivelled up and down from a braced couple of poles each end, and there was a long, narrow notched board to push the wire high into the sky so it didn't all sag towards the grass underneath.

I'd watch mum lift up the sheets and peg them to the outside wires and see them start to move in the breeze. She had a system a bit like the firewood but in reverse: she'd start with the big things and end up with the little ones like socks and pants on the inside wires. She was always careful to match up the socks and peg them next to each other. Then the exciting thing would be to get the prop and fit the notch in the centre of one of the outside wires, usually the one near the back fence. After that, she'd push it as high into the air as it would go and jam the point on the other end into the lawn. That made the swivel boards at the end tilt, and there she was, standing back admiring her slanting bank of washing ready to catch the sun and the wind.

I liked helping with the washing and the hanging up while the other two were perhaps playing nearby or inside. It was a good chance to be just me with Mum. For once, I wasn't pushed to the outside by the needs of smaller children and I was big enough to actually do something with her and share the experience with her.

The garden became beautifully full and abundant as the years went by. By the time I was a young adult, Mum had started gardening herself, and she became really good with roses. After a visit, we would drive back to Melbourne with a big bunch of mixed roses perfuming the car.

Later, when I had my own children, I loved returning to our Eaglehawk house and garden. My children slept in the same beds in the same bedroom as I had, under the same pretty green-and-white lily of the valley bedspreads that had been specially ordered by Mum. In the garden, the swing and the Easter bees were still there; the mulberry tree had subsided further and was even easier to climb, and the children rode their bikes down the drive and out on to the street, just as I had done. In our adult life, Mum always made the house calm and beautiful, and we children cherished it, the garden and her.

On a map of my childhood world, an X marks my home, the centre of my world. The house and garden are full of memories which surface, like islands from the sea. Some islands are steeply jutting, born of fire but with hearts of stone. They now lie bleak and dormant, with the occasional threat of volcanic spitting. Other isles are gentle sunlit places of abundance and happiness. The sea of everyday life surrounds these peaks of memory, bathing them in the repetitive and protective nourishment of daily life: meals and bedtimes, drying the dishes, talking in the kitchen, quietly reading or playing in the garden.

Chapter Six
Cubbies and Bonfires

Between the garage and the back fence was a bit of non-gardened backyard which couldn't be seen from the back door. That made it a good place for building cubbies.

The back fence was now 'the Buffaloes' fence'. When I was about eight, the old mattress factory on the block behind us was suddenly occupied again. An ornate façade appeared, embossed with the large letters RAOB. Mum said that the letters stood for a club called the Royal Antediluvian Order of Buffaloes. This was pretty funny, and it was even stranger when I learnt that it was a club for men only. I loved the word 'antediluvian' and had to go and look it up and keep saying it at any opportunity. Everyone now called the building 'the Buffaloes', hence the Buffaloes' fence.

By the time I was about ten, I had scrounged enough old corrugated iron and bits of building wood from the Buffaloes' old stables to have built a succession of lean-to cubbies against this back fence. I had tried a tree house in the pear tree, but that didn't really work because I couldn't make the floor sit flat.

My best cubby house ever was tucked in the corner of the Buffaloes' fence at the back and the neighbours' fence at the side. They had a very high wooden side fence and the Buffaloes' fence was high enough for me to use the horizontal runner bit of wood that they nailed the palings to, as a ledge to support my roof timbers. I dug holes to put my corner posts in, attached cross-beams and nailed the roof timbers to them. I then nailed the corrugated iron to these timbers to set up a roof gently sloping away from the fence. I allowed a bit of an overhang so it wouldn't make the walls wet. I was lucky to find some Masonite for the front wall, which I made windowless. The side wall was made of a smaller bit of Masonite which didn't reach to the roof and left a gap under the overhanging roof for a long narrow window.

It was a square, quite watertight building that I could actually stand up in. I'd better not start growing! It was even strong enough for me to be able to walk on its roof.

Now for the inside, I scavenged some old lino from somewhere and laid it on the floor. It was very exciting to have a blue-and-pink floral floor covering. On Mum's sewing machine, I made a curtain that could draw across the window. I nailed some more material above the narrow entrance on the side fence to make a long door curtain. It was now snug and secret.

I built a bench to sit on under the window – did it have cushions? At the rate I was going, I wouldn't be surprised. Then I made some shelves from wooden fruit boxes stacked against the Buffaloes' fence. The glory of those shelves was enhanced by some coloured hessian which I tacked in front of a couple of them.

It was an excellent cubby. It was satisfying to be in it when it rained and not have the roof leak. Sometimes after a lot of rain, water would come in from the side on to the floor, and I'd have to mop it up, but that was the wonder of lino, it came up shiny and better. I kept some books in there and enjoyed reading quietly, especially my comics.

Then I found some candles. Wouldn't they be wonderful, glowing away on a shelf behind the coloured hessian curtains? I did feel there was something a bit wrong about this idea, but it was too good to resist, and anyway, I'd be careful. I set them up, standing on blobs of melted wax. It was good fun playing with the candles, and I thought the cubby looked beautiful with the extra decoration. But there was always something missing – darkness!

So one evening after dinner, when it was just a little bit dark, we all went to play in the cubby, and I lit the candles behind the curtains. They flickered and danced, and we sat and admired them and moved them around to better places on their shelves. We went outside to see if we could see the candle light through the window curtains. No. Not really.

Yes! The cubby flickered.

No! It looked a bit big for a candle.

I raced inside. Richie and Jane squeezed in behind me. A corner of hessian had caught fire. The little candle flame had transformed itself into a licking, adventurous tongue of fire. Long and yellow, it climbed up the hessian, leaving a crimson base of glowing crisscross weave. There were trails of black smoke. I flapped and banged at it but couldn't stop the flame growing. By now, it had eaten the entire lower curtain and was reaching for the one above.

'Run and tell Mum.'

'Get some water.'

'Where's the hose?'

'Where's the bucket?'

I was useless and helpless. I couldn't find anything to carry enough water in. I think Mum and Dad might have been trying to untangle the hose. You could hear and smell the fire now. I was really frightened.

'You stupid kids!' yelled a voice from the top of the Brown's fence. Les was up there looking down. He vanished. Soon, an arc of water rose above the fence. It splashed around a bit while Les climbed up his ladder until he could stand and hose the fire out.

The whole thing was mortifying on a number of counts.

First, I had set fire to my dear cubby. Second, I couldn't put the fire out. Third, my parents were standing uselessly in a tangle of hose nowhere near the fire. Fourth, we had to be rescued by neighbours who weren't too keen on the cubby in that corner anyway. Fifth, I had to pull the burnt cubby down.

As far as choices were concerned, the combination of candles and hessian was definitely not a good decision. Possibly, I could have got away with just candles!

However, not to be discouraged, during the next school holidays, when I was wondering what do, I remembered that during some other holidays, some kids from up the back street and I had dug a deep rectangular hole up at the end of their backyard. School had gone back before we could do anything more with it.

I decided that I would make an underground cubby. I dug and dug up there behind the garage, making a grave-like hole that I could cover with a piece of old corrugated iron I still had from the burnt cubby. It was deep enough for two of us to sit in and I dug out little alcoves to put candles in. At least those walls wouldn't catch fire. The orange clay was cool and pleasant to sit on and lean against but that was about all we could do in it. This was during one of the winter school holidays, and of course, it rained. One wet morning, Dad called us up to look at the cubby. He'd pulled off the iron, and there it stood, a hole half full of orangey-brown water. I stood and looked at it. It didn't seem too bad to have to fill it in as it had been more fun to make than play in.

We also liked building bonfires. There was a vacant block of land in the middle of Church Street about six houses down from ours and opposite the street down to the park. We must have picked up that this was the place to build 'the' bonfire and somehow picked up when it was time to start building it. Maybe, one day, we saw that some big branches or wood rubbish had been put there. It was enough to get us going back to our sheds to find some rope and the axe. Sometimes, it would just be Jane, Rich and me, sometimes just me, and sometimes other kids from the street would appear. Then we'd go up the hill to the bush near the cemetery and golf course and pine plantation. There was a lot of Chinese scrub growing there, and I liked it because it had a really nice smell. The bushes were about our height or a bit taller, and I liked cutting them down near the base with the axe. It was fun to chop down a bush instead of splitting firewood. When we'd cut a pile, I'd line them up with their little trunks all clumped together and then use the rope to tie them tightly ready for the hard bit of dragging them home. They were a heavy load, and at the start, bits would fall out and have to be retied. We took turns dragging the load up past the cemetery to the top of our hill. From there, it was downhill and easier. The scrub left a smooth path behind us on which you could walk and make footprint patterns – that is, if you weren't the one towing.

We'd get to the block, hot and thirsty, drag the load up to the heap and throw it on. Over the years, I learnt to leave some light bushy bits on the outside, where they were easy to light and catch, and put the trunks into the centre. Occasionally, we'd see a man come with a trailer and throw some wood on to the heap. Sometimes, the bonnie would grow miraculously almost overnight, but as a rule we would do quite a few trips up to the bush to get our scrub. The closer to the time, the more excited we got. I'd go down to look at it and prod at it and make it good. Others would do the same. A dad would appear with a shovel and scrape away a clear space around its base.

One year, someone put a guy on the top to burn. I knew about Guy Fawkes, and I knew it was meant to be fun, but I felt a bit uneasy about the idea of burning even a pretend person. The figure looked grotesque and crumpled lying up there at the top, not at all like an angel or star on the top of a Christmas tree.

Somehow, we knew not to put paper in the bonfire until the actual night. And we also knew what time to go down there. The families would gather as it got darker and darker, and we ran around getting more and more excited and fidgety. The grown-ups took charge. Crumpled newspaper was stuffed into the waiting bonfire and finally, the papers were lit. Little fires crept out in the dark and climbed up the bushy walls. The scrub hissed and crackled and sparked as it burnt and helped the heavier wood and leaves ignite. We moved further and further back as the fire became orange and hot and roared into the sky. Faces were lit golden and people were happy. We became quiet as we watched the huge heap, which had been more than twice my height, gradually sink into an incandescent cauldron.

Then it was time for fireworks. We'd all been spending our pocket money on fireworks from Mundy's, who had a special counter of them for Guy Fawkes Day and the other bonfire night: was it Empire Day?

I liked the ones you set on the ground, like fountains, which shot up streams of changing colour safely in front of us. Rockets seemed to be a bit unreliable and sometimes worked well but often just shot off and did nothing much. There was too much fuss and bother with setting them safely and accurately.

I liked the red bangers, going from the little Tom Thumbs – one of which you could hold gingerly by its very end while it exploded – up to the big fat bungers. I was a bit scared of those huge ones but liked the way jumping jacks jumped and exploded around us at random. We all loved sparklers, which were safe and fun to run around with making sparkly patterns against the darkness.

The fireworks would run out, the bonnie would be burning very low, the little kids would be grizzling and it would be time to go home.

I suppose that each year I remembered more of what had happened in the past and was quicker to jump into action. It didn't only happen with the bonfires but with switches of games from footie to cricket, from skipping to hopscotch, from swap cards to marbles. What I like, in thinking about this, is the way that the neighbourhood signals floated in the air ready for us to pick up and respond to.

Chapter Seven
Swimming

Throughout childhood, the seasons changed slowly and winter seemed to last forever. Finally, one Saturday at home on a warm, sunny spring morning, I realised it was warm enough for shorts. I found some at the bottom of my drawer, pulled off my long winter pants and found that last year's shorts still fitted me. I looked down at the airy whiteness of my legs and felt excited about getting them brown over summer. Then I remembered that the baths might be filling soon. I couldn't wait to get outside. As soon as I'd had breakfast, I was out to the garage for my bike. I was still too small to sit on the seat. I wheeled it across the dirt floor and out to the driveway.

'Bye, Mum.'

I scooted off past the kitchen window and the grevillea that the honey eaters visited, wheels crunching on the gravel drive, did a good skiddy brake before the footpath – no old ladies on bikes or cars in sight, over the gutter bridge and down to the baths. Past the peppercorn trees on the corner, past Miss Cook's, and now I did have to pause and look as I crossed Victoria Street, which often had cars on it. Still standing on the pedals with the seat nudging my back, I rolled and bumped across the corrugations down the little hill to the park, slalomed through the white posts and turned right to the baths.

'Ah! They're still empty.' I rode right up to the shallow end where the big pipe let in the water. Not a trickle.

The waterless hole stretched out beside the lake. The brown lake glittered but the baths' grey, sandy bottom was warm and dry. The concrete side walls baked in the sun. I jumped about a foot down onto the sand in the shallow end and walked over to the post and chain fence separating the bubby pool from the big pool. I ducked under the chain and wondered about bringing the bike down to ride on the bottom of the baths. No, the sand was too soft.

I walked towards the deep end, and about halfway there, my head was below the concrete edges. I'd be out of my depth by now if the pool were full. It was very quiet. I couldn't see the lake any more but ahead, in the distance, under the deep end diving board was a small pool of stagnant water. I walked under the side diving board which most of us played on and continued towards the end.

Now I was feeling a bit nervous. I'd reached the deep end and the sand had changed to a damper sort of silt as I approached the water. The muddy edges sloped steeply into the murk. I saw dog prints in them but no people's footprints. The water was thick and smelly. I turned around to look for my bike which was now a long way away. No one was in the park or the old bandstand or playground. I wouldn't have been able to get to the deep board's ladder if someone scary came along – it was the other side of the stagnant water. I checked the side diving board's ladder whose steps I saw didn't go all the way down. At least the bottom rungs were about shoulder height so I could climb up it if I'd had to.

'Hmm!' I started walking back to my bike, not exploring this time. I felt better as I 'surfaced', even though it was through air, not water. It was a relief to see the grassy banks and the old rowing club come into view. I hadn't expected that stroll on the bottom of the pool to feel so threatening.

I sat by the bike and longed for fast, clean, flowing water

to emerge so that I could have a swim. All the water around Eaglehawk was still and brown. The lake was topped up with the overflow from the baths. Eaglehawk Creek was not really flowing. Judging by the other creeks around, it probably had still, dark water lying in small pools at the bottom of high banks. I knew from books that The Famous Five and Ratty could sit on soft grass beside running streams with water near the top of the banks. I was so envious of them being able to have all that watery softness.

You could only see the rim of the round pipe if you knelt down and looked into the dark cavity behind the flat concrete slab. I remembered from last year that, when the water came, the slab smoothed it into a wide, gleaming curve. A little river had formed and flowed down the centre of the baths to join the remains of last year's water.

I didn't understand where this water came from. Who decided to make it come? How did they know when to do it? And how did they do it? Was there a big tap somewhere? I just had to wait.

When the pool was finally filled for summer, I loved riding my bike down the couple of blocks, propping it against the creek fence, taking myself into the change rooms, rolling my clothes into a little bundle and then finding a nice place on the grass by the pool to leave them with my towel. Sometimes, I would ride down just in bathers with my towel round my neck. It was a lot of fun playing and jumping and diving, and there was usually someone there I knew, but it didn't matter if there wasn't.

On another hot day in early summer, when I was a couple of years older and, again, before the pool was filled, our grade five girls were having a school picnic day at the Eaglehawk Park. I was the only girl in the school who lived in Eaglehawk and was surprised and proud that we were all coming out to my park for the day. It was surprising all round: we didn't usually have picnics, and nice girls certainly didn't come out to Eaglehawk, which was poor and a bit rough by Bendigo's standards.

I had needed to get special permission not to have to come in to school and then go out to Eaglehawk again. I met my classmates and Miss Cure at the terminus tram stop. We entered the park through the ornate wrought iron gates and walked past the Eaglehawk statues on their columns. I showed my classmates the gardened section – Canterbury Gardens, although none of us referred to them as such – which had lawns, flowerbeds and big European trees. I didn't point out the lovers' lane to Miss Cure. We could all see the Borough footy ground to the left, and then in front of us, through the white wooden fence at the end, stretched the 'big' bit of the park with the lake and the pool.

The huge gaping sandy hole in the ground with concrete edges was our pool, waiting to be filled for summer. Bendigo people thought it was dirty, but it didn't smell, nor did we get sick.

Next to it, separated by a straight earth wall was Lake Neangar with its almost disused rowing club shed. It had been excavated in 1883 by men using picks and shovels, but as children, we didn't know anything about that. Councils didn't put up information boards back then. There was a big overflow down to the creek on the side and a little overflow at the far end. Sometimes, water would flow over down into the creek and the rough ground on the other side of the road where all the bull rushes were. Near the swimming pool outlet into the lake, you could sit in a willow tree which leant over the water and take your shoes and socks off to dangle your feet in the brown, cool water.

We played for a bit in the park and then had our lunch in the grassy shade.

Suddenly, we ran out of things to do. During the morning, I had been a bit disappointed that the thrill of leaping off the swings into the sand didn't catch on with my classmates.

'Come and look at the lake.'

'Be careful, girls!'

The lake had a little gravelly shore at one point, and we clustered there like butterflies around a puddle, in our seersucker uniform dresses, just looking at the water. The sun was hot. It was obvious to have a paddle. Even the idea felt a bit naughty, and not all of us took the step of taking off our brown lace-up shoes and socks to test the prickly gravel with our soft winter feet.

The water felt wonderful and cool. I stepped a little deeper where the gravel mixed with some mud and was softer underfoot. Brown water crept higher and higher up my legs. I tucked my dress into my brown Cottontail panties and waded out as far as I could without getting them wet. The lake water had been lying there under the early summer sun for long enough to be pleasantly not cold. I loved feeling the water lapping against my legs. I didn't like the feel of the mud underfoot though and was a bit scared of treading on a broken bottle or yabbie.

I wanted to feel this water all over my body, on my head and face, and to float and bob and swim in it. I hadn't had a swim since last autumn. I'd never swum in the lake. Why not now? The girls were there, so I wouldn't be completely alone. I knew I could swim well. I didn't think there were any tree snags in there. Miss Cure would be cross, but that wouldn't be too bad. Mum wouldn't mind. The uniform would wash. And what a funny thing it would be to do. How could I resist it?

I didn't. It felt odd to be swimming in clothes, but they were light and my skirt was already tucked into my pants. I swam out a bit towards the middle, enjoyed being out of my depth, bobbed around a bit looking back and waving at the now screaming and laughing girls and decided to set off for the rowing shed ramp about fifty yards away.

So there I was, in the lake, in my clothes, happily swimming parallel to the shore about twenty yards out and heading towards the old rowing shed. Grade five were on the shore in a state of mixed hilarity and anxious excitement. Still no sight of Miss Cure. Then, on the side, as I was taking my breath between strokes, I saw another group approaching from the gardens' end. That must be Miss Cure and the good girls.

I stopped and looked, treading water. Miss Cure was shouting something and beckoning me in. I yelled that I would get out at the ramp and swam on. Next to the rowing ramp, there was quite a reception committee. I hoisted myself on to the wet, slimy boards, shook my dress out, concentrated on walking up without slipping and jumped ashore.

Well, I suppose I got into trouble at school. I don't remember and it didn't matter. I had had my first swim of summer, in the lake, in my clothes and, technically, while at school.

At about that time, I started hanging around the milk bar up the street, where I could buy a threepenny glass of lime cordial and lemonade. Mr Masters and his wife, who 'wasn't well', had recently moved to Eaglehawk and made the old milk bar at the top of our street really nice. He was a large friendly man with a lot of patience as we kids chose the lollies for our threepenny bags of sweets. Many, like Spearmint Leaves, were four a penny, and he didn't mind you having two of them and, say, two Choc Balls for one penny's worth. Actually, lolly buying must have sharpened up our arithmetic no end!

I liked the fizzy cordial idea. It meant that I could stay in the shop and sit on a stool while I drank it very slowly and watched Mr Masters serve customers. He would sometimes chat to me in quiet moments and occasionally take me through the curtain separating the shop from his living room at the back to say hello to his wife. She would be sitting by the fireplace, facing the window opening on to the brick wall of the shop next door. She was nice to me, but I didn't know what to say to her.

Once, towards the end of the day, a customer, an older man, jerked his head at me after he'd bought his cigarettes and asked, 'What's she doing here?' I was embarrassed, but Mr Masters just said something like, 'Oh, she's all right', and that seemed to do.

Another afternoon when it was getting a bit late, Mr Masters said, 'Isn't it time for your dinner?'

'Oh, yes. Goodbye.'

I slid off the stool where I had been perched with my empty glass sitting amongst the lolly jars on the counter beside me.

Out the door and past the two empty shops, look right and left and run across the road and tram track into Church Street. The St Peter's corner on my right was quiet and empty with nothing going on in the old sandstone hall at this time of day. I trotted down the hill towards home a couple of hundred yards away to practise my running.

A couple of days before, I had burst into the milk bar, breathless and excited.

'I've run all the way up here!'

'Oh. That's nothing. You should be able run further than that,' Mr

Masters had replied and continued drying up the milkshake glasses. That was a bit deflating so I had resolved to do better.

I turned into our drive and looked through the lit-up kitchen window as I ran past, and there was Mum at the bench and Pa already sitting at the table. The rest weren't in sight, so I wasn't late. Maybe Mr Masters was a bit sick of me being in the shop.

The shop was friendly and quiet compared to home, and I liked the idea of knowing a man who had been a high diver for Australia in the 1936 Berlin Olympic Games. He was an exotic person to drift ashore in Eaglehawk in the early 1950s.

One afternoon during the school holidays, he appeared at the baths. He strolled up to the board in his bathers, with a towel over his shoulder, and watched the kids diving and bombing for a while.

'Look! It's Mr Masters!'

We stood around watching and hoping we would see this famous man dive. Yes, we would! He dropped his towel and moved into the queue. His body was strong and muscly and looked very different from most of the dad's bodies that we saw at the baths. The queue fell away.

Mr Masters stepped on to the back of the board and stood there, in a special way. He stood tall and still and then walked down the board strongly and deliberately, paused and lifted one knee high before bringing it down hard and making the board bend further than we'd ever seen. His arms reached out and his body shot into the air, straight and smooth. Then he curved into a swallow dive. The water received him with barely a splash. He surfaced, flicked his hair aside and swam powerfully and smoothly to the side, flipped himself out and stood there dripping.

This was the first time that I'd seen anything like that stylised preparation and the seemingly effortless performance. I could see the theatrical nature of the dive but also realised that the rather odd walking and standing was an important part of the actual time in the air. In that dive, Mr Masters had shown my eight-year-old self something extraordinary. It was the magnificent extension of what we all just did and played around with. I realised that the beauty of the dive with its power and control didn't just happen. I knew that this was something he had worked at. The idea that people could do something like that was exciting. I knew about ballet dancers and piano players, but this was something from my playing, watery world, which was real and direct. It was there, in front of me.

He did a few more dives, one with a tight curled somersault, and then stood around giving a few tips to the kids who were game enough to get on the board after him. After that, he came down to the pool a few times in the later afternoon and somehow started doing a little low-key swimming coaching. I loved that and began to develop a smoother freestyle stroke.

Then we learnt that he was going to have a swimming carnival at our baths. There would be races and a diving competition, and he would give an exhibition of diving. I was really excited. On the carnival day, we found the pool transformed. There were coloured flags strung around, a loudspeaker set up and music playing. Men organised us kids into groups for our races. We had to swim across the pool at its widest part. I knew I'd be able to do that.

We got lined up on the concrete edge, there was some sort of starting signal, and away we went. I could hear the loudspeaker blaring as I splashed my way across the pool and eventually landed up way over to the right – a very diagonal course. I didn't know what to do next as it was all a bit confusing, but it turned out that I'd won the race. Mum later said that everyone was laughing, but in a nice way, at this little kid racing off to the side but still in front. Winning was a bit spoilt by the idea of being laughed at.

Back at the milk bar, Mr Masters talked about swimming and training. I liked the idea of doing something you enjoyed and making yourself get better at it. He must have talked to Mum about the Bendigo Swimming Club and how I could go in races there. And that was how I found myself at the Bendigo Baths one afternoon after school waiting to do a time trial to get a handicap for the club's Sunday morning races. I'd never been in the Bendigo Baths before, but I had previously seen from the car that they were in an enclosure in a big lake. Mum took me in through the entrance, and we found Mr Monaghan, the club president. I had to stand on the wet wooden platform at the shallow end and wait for the starting signal.

'On your mark! Get set! Go!'

Off I dived, racing up the pool, trying really hard, not quite knowing where I was going and lifting my head up from time to time to see where I was. I was to swim fifty-five yards up to the diving tower. It was hard to keep going because there were a lot of people swimming that afternoon, and it was all new to me. I swam out past the playing kids, saw the white tower as I turned to breathe and stopped in the middle of all this water stretching in all directions. I saw Mr Monaghan standing with his stop watch in his hand near the diving boards so swam over to him.

'Good girl. Now go over to the ladies' side and see me back at the start.'

So I swam over to the ladies side, climbed out and ran down to the start. Mr Monaghan told me that I had done 60 seconds and I'd be racing in the Under 12s on Sunday morning. I was nine, but Under 12 was as young as they went.

It was pretty special on Sunday because I was allowed to miss church and Sunday School. Mum didn't know what to do with my plaits to keep them out of the way while I swam and eventually decided to pin them up on the top of my head. She dropped me off at the pool and headed off back to church.

When my race came, it was the first of the morning because Under 12 was the youngest, and the girls always went before the boys' equivalent age race. They had floated a white wooden railing across the end at fifty-five yards so I knew I would have something to stop me from swimming out into the big lake. We were lined up on the edge in order according to our handicap. I was given a number to remember and told that when the starter counted up to that number I was to dive in and start racing. I stood there, listening hard above the splashes of each girl diving in according to her handicap, hoping I wouldn't miss my number.

Here it was. I dived in and set off as fast as I could trying to catch up to the others. But the pinned up plaits were a disaster. My dive had knocked the bobby pins askew, and the plaits started creeping down over my eyes and face. Mum had tied the ends together, so I ended the race with the plaits down under my chin. I also ended up way over to the side having swum another diagonal course. Where were the others? I looked and they were still coming up the pool.

After the races were finished, we all crowded into the club house room, and the men called out our times. I had knocked fifteen seconds off my time.

For quite a time, I only went to the Bendigo Baths on Sunday mornings for the races. I loved that I was allowed to swim and not have to go to church and Sunday School during summer. I realise now that Mum must have done quite a lot of juggling to make sure she, not Dad, had the car at that time, and that my brother and sister were being looked after. Actually, they were probably in Sunday School.

When I was a bit older and had made friends with the other swimmers, I would go back into the baths on the Sunday afternoon tram. The trams didn't run on Sunday morning and only left the depot at 2 pm. The first one reached Eaglehawk at 2.30, meaning that it would be three o'clock before I could get back into the baths, which were about a ten-minute walk from the tram stop. Still, it was worth it on a hot day. Gradually, over the years, I stopped going to the Eaglehawk Baths during the summer school holidays, and I caught the tram in to Bendigo.

The Bendigo Municipal Baths were paying baths, unlike Eaglehawk and California Gully where you just went and jumped in the water. Three sides of cream-painted weatherboard buildings enclosed a fifty-five-yard by about twenty-yard stretch of water within a large, deep dammed-up lake. Strangely, this lake was on top of the hill that rose from Rosalind Park adjoining the Bendigo shops. It was surrounded by schools, an oval, lawn tennis courts and the houses across the road.

You entered the Muni (pronounced Muney) Baths under a sort of dome on the corner of the buildings. Len, the superintendent, sat in an office to the left, and in the early days before I got a season ticket, I would pay him, clank through a turnstile and turn left to the ladies changing rooms. The gents changing rooms faced the ladies across the water and the low wooden deck at the shallow end joined the two. Both the ladies and the gents had wide wooden decking with a lower ledge to sit on just above water level. We each had a one-metre diving board. We weren't allowed on the gents' side, and they certainly weren't allowed on ours. We were always very suspicious that boys might be quietly swimming under our change rooms and looking up through the gaps in the floor boards. Neutral territory was the landward decking between them both at the shallow end and the high diving area at the deep end of the gents.

One Christmas, I was desperate for a blow-up rubber shark floatie toy I'd seen in one of the Bendigo shops. Sharkie came to me in the pillowcase at the end of my bed on Christmas morning. It was dark red, with pointy white teeth painted on and a sort of hole in the middle for me to sit in and paddle around. I really wanted to show it off at the baths and play with it but that was tricky because there was a rule: no inflatable tubes or toys. I thought I'd try my luck. So, on Boxing Day, my inflated shark and I approached the gate. I looked up at Len behind the counter. Len said that I wasn't allowed to take it in because of the rule. I said things like 'You know I can swim' and 'Please!' and 'Just this once' and 'There's hardly anyone here.'

Very kindly, he relented, and my shark and I took to the water. I loved playing in him, but it wasn't as much fun as I'd hoped. My friends weren't there, and I felt a bit guilty and self-conscious bobbing around in the nearly empty pool by myself.

It was much more fun down at the Eaglehawk Pool when I took Sharkie down there. No one cared whether you were safe or not, and the shark was the envy of all the kids. On the other hand, seeing the inflated inner tubes the other kids were using made me a bit self-conscious.

The Bendigo Pool had a lot of diving boards. There was a very bouncy three-metre diving board and, beside it, a tall, narrow, white wooden tower. This had a ladder up the back which led first to the small five-metre platform and then stretched up further to the seven-and-a-half-metre ledge and finally reached the frightening ten-metre platform, which jutted out over those below it. We weren't really allowed to just climb up to the top if we weren't going to jump, so I only went up there very occasionally when the baths were quiet. Len didn't seem to mind that. Otherwise, he'd yell at you over the loudspeaker.

It was a long, vertical climb up the wooden ladder. I was very aware that I had to grip hard and hold my weight. Eventually, I'd get to the top and step on to the platform. Ohh! It was such a long way down. I'd be careful to stand in the middle or hang on to the railing. The top of the tower felt small and foundationless and sometimes shook a bit. I felt bare and exposed, so high in the air, and defenceless, clad only in wet Speedos. It was hard to make myself walk to the edge and stand there. I would have been a small figure up there with the afternoon sun on my back. It was enough to be there, and I was quite happy to make way if any big boys or young men came up to leap and bomb.

I never did jump off the tower but came close to it one evening when I was about fourteen. I stood and looked for a long time as the baths got quieter and quieter and the sun dropped lower and lower behind me. Finally, I stepped back and climbed down. Seven and a half metres was quite enough to jump from. The five-metre platform was easy, but I never liked diving from it. I wasn't a good diver and didn't have the knack of tucking my head in enough not to bang it when I hit the water.

Out in the open water past the diving tower was the wooden 'raft', which wasn't really a raft as it was on piles. The platform was neutral territory and very popular with the older kids and adults to bask on. I'd swim out and sort of bob around in the water like a baby seal at the edge, but if I was by myself, I was too shy to climb aboard.

Even further, one hundred yards from the shallow end of the pool, was the water polo pool. I would set off through the open water past the diving tower to reach it. It always felt a bit of a lonely swim, even if swimming out with others. The water felt bottomless: it was so deep and had a different, still quality compared to the choppiness of the water in the edged baths. The sun's light refracted greenly down to browny-black.

The water polo pool was another rectangular wooden structure painted white and built in deep water. There was a goal net at each end and ledges to sit on. On Sunday afternoons, after the club races in the morning, we'd swim out to the water polo pool to cheer on our Bendigo Baths team against other local teams. It was yet another 'men only' sport, but I would have liked to play it.

I had a life of my own at the Bendigo Baths. I could get there by myself by tram. My friends there were completely different from the ones at school or Eaglehawk or church. We all enjoyed chasing and ducking and jumping and bombing. We'd play 'keeping's off' when we were allowed to have a water polo ball in the pool. I liked that because it was a bit like water polo, and it was fun to learn how to swim and shepherd the ball away from the others and then throw it to a team member. I liked having boys to play with. They were funny and cheerful and energetic.

When I was about ten or eleven, I made a friend at the club. After swimming, we would go back to her house a couple of blocks from the pool, walk in through the back gate and into the kitchen, which was dark and cool. Her mother would give us glasses of cordial with ice blocks and serve us cake. She made really nice orange cakes. We would sit at the laminex kitchen table and eat and eat, and drink and drink. I loved having so much sweet food. A few times, she was out but still left cake for us. Later, I would walk to the tram stop, hop on the tram full of people coming home from work and get home in time for dinner.

I don't think we did any training at all for our races when I was in the Under 12s and 14s. Playing seemed to be enough to make us fit and strong.

The club went to the Castlemaine Pool, about thirty miles away, by bus one Saturday for some races. I was ten and really didn't have a clue about what was happening but was excited to go to Castlemaine because they had the only chlorinated baths in the district. I'd been there a couple of times when Mum took us. I'd never been on a bus before. It was full of club members and officials like Mr Monaghan, now Mr Mon, and his brother, the other Mr Mon, who was the father of my friend. The big kids sat up the back and the officials and their wives at the front. I found a seat somewhere near the front.

It was a bit confusing when we got there, but I went and got changed and hung around with the other kids on the thick green grass beside the pool. Someone came and took me to the end of the pool when my race came on. This wasn't a handicap because these were championships. I lined up in front of a lane with the other girls, got a bit of a fright when the starting gun went off and swam the race. The unfamiliar chlorine made my eyes sting, but I kept straight thanks to the floating lane ropes and the line on the bottom of the pool. I got to the end, climbed out and went back to my towel. I was sitting there happily with all the announcements and races swirling around, when later in the afternoon, one of the officials came and collected me. He told me that I was in a 'final' and I'd need to swim another race and to try and win it. Well, I always tried to win, but this seemed to be special. So off I dived and swam as hard as I could in the choppy water. At the end, I was about to go back again to my towel on the grass when someone stopped me and said, 'No. Wait here.' I then heard, 'Elizabeth Trembath,' announced over the loudspeaker and was led to a sort of stepped platform marked 1, 2, 3. I was told to get on to 3 and was given a certificate for third place in the Central Victorian Girls' Under 12 Swimming Championships. How surprising and exciting!

It was a bit strange after the swimming had finished. We all got on the bus again and were taken down to the Castlemaine Main Street so we could buy something for our dinner. I didn't know what to do, really. Everyone else went off to the cafes and fish and chip shops. I saw where the officials went – into a pub for a drink and their dinner. I must have bought something to eat and walked up and down the street, which was getting a bit grey and dark and empty. I thought I would wait outside the pub for the grown-ups. This didn't feel too good as pubs had a very bad name in our family. People who went to pubs were drunks! So I just stood there. Then one of the wives came out to me. Children weren't allowed in pubs, but she said that they wouldn't be long and we'd be going home soon. When they came out, they weren't horrible and drunk. They were very cheerful and friendly and gathered me up and took me back to the bus.

It was dark as we drove home. People sang, and I was very happy.

We went on many of these bus trips away from Eaglehawk over the years, and I liked visiting and swimming in the various pools. At Echuca, we swam in the brown-green water of the Murray in a short stretch of the river between two grey bleached piers jutting into the stream. We'd get a whoosh with the current downstream but had to push hard against it upstream. Tongala, in the irrigated dairy areas to the north of Bendigo, had a strongly chlorinated pool in a sort of lush oasis of thick green grass and trees. What a contrast that was to the dry end-of-summer landscape we had just driven through. Shepparton, also to the north, was rather like Bendigo, with its official pool fenced off in a lake. I was never as unaware and confused as on that first bus trip to Castlemaine and came to enjoy wandering around the streets after the carnivals with a group of friends, eating fish and chips and waiting for the bus to drive us home.

I liked playing with the other kids and hanging around the pool with them. By the time I was about eleven, I had stopped playing so much with the Eaglehawk boys on the street and was getting to know the swimming club boys. I enjoyed mucking around with them, laughing and learning to make jokes. There was something cheerful about boys, I thought.

They were very good at making jokes, and I still laugh at the memory of the sign at the baths that said something like, 'Boisterous Behaviour Will Not Be Tolerated'. One afternoon, we were hanging around near the sign after training when Cedge, short for Cedric, short for Geoff, out of the blue said, 'What about *girlsterous* behaviour! Us boys are always blamed for everything!'

Girlsterous behaviour is a lot of fun.

I was happy racing and later on, training. I liked finessing my stroke and developing my strength. Being in a club where we all shared something we loved gave me a sense of belonging and being appreciated and liked. The repetition of training was satisfying, and I became stronger and faster and won races. I'm glad to have experienced that early discipline and persistence, which created a sort of template for adult life. For the last few years, I've been learning tango, and I've enjoyed re-engaging with an awareness of the physicality of my body, developing skills and finding pleasure in refining movements.

The old freshwater Eaglehawk Baths are no longer. An outdoor chlorinated Olympic pool was built on the site, and later the pool was enclosed. People can now swim all year round. The seasonality of swimming has gone

Although I'm not so keen on swimming laps, I love swimming in natural water. I'm 'collecting' swims in oceans and seas in a low-key sort of way and savour the different qualities of the water. The warm, calm inky blue of the waters off Dubrovnik are gentle and luxurious compared to the 'bracing' gasp-making waters of the surf on Victoria's coastline. Inland waters have their own charms, and there's a certain frisson to swimming in 'crocodile free' waterholes in Australia's Northern Territory.

July, 2014

Nick and I arrived at our rented cottage by the river, unpacked, looked around and I decided that I really wanted a swim.

I sat on the end of the nearby wooden jetty. Each side, rowing boats and small motor boats jostled quietly on their mooring ropes. Across the Thames, the sloping beach of the old ferry landing place was now empty. The dogs, horses, bikes, children and their parents had gone home at the end of the long hot afternoon.

About a metre under my feet, I could see the yellow, gravelly bottom and one large rock. I wished I was wearing reef sandals for this swimming adventure and sat and dithered for a while wondering if it would be safe.

Right! It's time to do it!

Aah! My feet touched bottom, the water came to just above my waist. The gravel was a bit slimy but alright, and there I was, standing in the Thames. The water was soft and cool, not even 'bracing', and I whooshed out away from the jetty over the dark, undulating waterweed. With feet off the bottom, I was weightless, floating and bobbing, and all the heat and humidity of the day vanished in that moment. I rolled onto my back, kicked and paddled, then ducked my head under to feel the water on my scalp. Now it was a proper swim with the cool water all over my head and my hair floating.

I had held my nose because I wasn't entirely sure of the cleanliness of the river. However, people had been swimming from the opposite bank, and now that I was in it, the water didn't smell, so I thought it would be safe enough. It did have a rather solid greenness as if it were packed with vitamised greenery like a very thin breakfast drink of kale and green leafy vegetables. Just then a blob of white and grey swan poo floated past at eye level. *Well,* I thought, *there's a lot of water to dilute that,* and swam out further towards the middle.

And there I found the living river. The current moved like a long engulfing muscle, pushing against the whole length of my body. In seconds, I had been taken down past the motor boats and the willow trees. Right! It was time to concentrate on swimming. I put my head down and swam hard against the current to level with the jetty and move out of the current to where Nick was now standing in the water.

I dropped my feet to the bottom and stood in chest-high water. The water there moved past me gently, and it was safe to float and kick and look around. The cottage that we were renting was just on the towpath about forty metres away upstream. Soon we'd get out, walk back along the towpath, shower and change and sit with a gin and tonic, amazed at what we'd just done.

This swim was sixty-three years after my Eaglehawk gutter swim. I'd often visited the UK with my English husband and had always wanted to stay in a house on the banks of the Thames, to see what it would be like to be so close to the water all the time. I wanted to live within the dream-like descriptions of the English river in The *Wind in the Willows*.

I will remember floating in that beautiful famous river and looking at eye level across to the banks where huge, soft green trees leaned right down to almost touch the water. I'll remember sharing the water with the two swans (in Europe, I have to fight not to say 'white' swans) who lived on that stretch of water and would occasionally make a regal visit to the banks of our cottage. At dusk, the flocks of Canada geese raced up and down just above the surface of the water like fighter planes, and their raucousness reminded me of the screeching racket made by Australia's sulphur-crested cockatoos.

In my delight at this Thames swim, I remembered my early childhood 'swim' in the flooded gutter at Eaglehawk. The pleasure and achievement felt very similar.

Chapter Eight
Beach Holidays

After Christmas each year we'd start longing for our beach holiday. Dad wanted his two weeks of holiday; Mum wanted a change and a bit of a rest, and we were all keen to see the sea and get away from the heat of Eaglehawk.

The drive to 'the beach' followed the same pattern each year. All of us would finally be in the car, with the suitcases full of clean, ironed clothes in the boot. Whichever place we went to was always over a hundred miles away, and we would have a picnic lunch on the way. The smallest child was in prime position between Mum and Dad, perched in a canvas seat hooked over the front bench seat. I sat behind Dad. The full car laboured up Big Hill, just outside Bendigo, and the rolling landscape opening in front of us at the top signalled that we were really on our way. The car had a rest as it rolled down the Calder Highway through the sheep paddocks and under the large gums beside the road.

We drove forever. On our drives to the sea, we left behind the browned off, dry and crackling inland landscape. We left the muddy water that lay flat in the Eaglehawk lake, and which we also saw in the still, dark pools of Bullock and Buckeye Creeks as we crossed them going down Big Hill.

Ahead of us was the open sea. I daydreamed about it as we drove. It was blue! It moved and had waves that hissed and foamed up on to the wet sand. The sand was clean, golden and crunchy underfoot unlike our soft, fine grey sand from the mines. The sea was huge and stretched forever out to a thin line where it met the sky. It was clean and fresh and smelt ... well, like the sea. Sometimes, the smell had the special 'under the pier' smell: cool, fresh and seaweedy.

I would remember the sand dunes waiting for me to climb and run down and the rocky bits of the beach that were fun to climb over. Sometimes, there were rock pools to look into containing a little underwater world of waving seaweeds and strange dark red blobs of what looked like jelly stuck on the rock walls. We would see little fish or sea snails crawling around in there.

Then there were tea tree tunnels leading to the beach. The sand, sheltered from the sun by the arching overhead branches, would be cool and soft under our bare feet. Sunny spots had us squealing and jumping onto patches of shade. The path curved through the twisted, hairy grey trunks until it opened out to the gold sand and blue sea ahead of us.

Often we stopped for a break at Bacchus Marsh (or Blackus Mask, as the mother of one of Richard's friends called it). It was a relief to enter Bacchus Marsh after the baking highway because there were avenues of huge green trees casting deep shade over the road. Even better than the shade tunnel was the Bacchus Marsh swimming pool with bright blue chlorinated water. If we were lucky, we were allowed a swim there, 'Just a quick one!' It was so good to jump into that water after hours of driving, and it made getting back into the oven of a car much easier.

Soon after Bacchus Marsh, we looked for the first sight of the sea. It was a competition to be the first to spot a streak of blue between the brown hills. 'I can see the sea!'

Then there was Geelong to get through. I got really anxious at this stage because Mum and Dad said things like, 'Is it this turning?' Or 'I don't think this is the road. Should we turn around?' I was scared of being lost. Once, they had to ask someone for directions, which was not only embarrassing but seemed to add to the confusion. Finally, I might hear something like, 'Ah, this looks right,' and settle down with relief. I wish I had known then that the confusion would always sort itself out and that we wouldn't be driving around Geelong all night.

One year at Geelong, we stopped for a break on the lawns leading down to the open sea baths, and I was allowed to have a swim in them. They looked strange and large. Huge grey posts like pier posts made an enclosure to swim in, and there were heavy grey board walkways. Most different was the way the water heaved and sank through the swimming enclosure, sucking and slapping around the posts. I saw some other kids jumping in and jumped in where they did. The sea felt bottomless, and when I opened my eyes under water, all I saw was blue. I wasn't used to being out of my depth in the sea, and I swam around feeling small, excited and nervous amidst all this alive and enveloping water. When Mum called me to get out, I climbed up the ladder through the water rising and falling around me, feeling just a bit relieved.

For a couple of years, we stayed at Ocean Grove in a house just across the road from a beautiful little tea tree tunnel to the beach. This beach was an ocean beach with huge golden sand dunes to run down. The sea roared and the waves were called 'surf'. This was so different from the bay beach at Dromana, another holiday place, where the water had been shallow and quiet, just like a giant kids' swimming pool. I loved learning what to do with these strong, active waves. They hissed and foamed and pushed me around, sometimes knocking me over even when it was only knee-deep. I learnt to look at the waves and pick the right time to push off with them. When I was little, I would just push off into the broken wave near the shore and enjoy the quick surge around my body, though I actually didn't get carried very far. Later, I would stand further out, look at the green roll of water approaching, see the little frothing, curving frill on the top and feel the pull towards the wave, and then leap into it, swimming hard to catch the right moment and spot to be carried forward with it.

It was even better when we were allowed to hire a surfboard for the day. These were long, flat plywood boards to lie on, about as wide as our bodies and curved up at the front like a ski. I loved them because they made it really easy to catch a wave and stay on it right up to being grounded on the sand. I learnt to lean and steer it and loved guiding it right up to where Mum was standing in the water.

Cold days meant that we went for a drive, and once we ended up somewhere with a pier to walk on. It was windy out there, making the sea slide and roll against the posts below us. Fishermen hunched amongst their buckets and rods. I looked down at the water, and there, on a low cross-beam barely above the waves, I saw a tangle of fishing line. Maybe if I got that, I could do some fishing. I climbed down to the beam, which now had water sploshing on it, and reached for the tangle of nylon line. I grabbed a handful and lifted it. It moved. It tugged and pulled.

'It's a fish!' I yelled.

Rich and Jane leaned over.

'A fish. Lizzie's caught a fish.'

I balanced and started to pull in the tugging, jerking line. Then on the surface burst a long black twisting body, thrashing and writhing. 'It's a snake. No, it's an eel!'

People looked over the top as I drew in the long strong body of a two-and-a-half-foot eel, which hung and twisted and flipped in the air. It was a bit precarious down there. How was I going to get up with this creature?

'Here, love, I'll take it for you,' said a voice from above. I reached up and handed the heavy line to the man and climbed back to the top, very excited. The eel lay there quietly, so he must have killed it for me while I was on my way up. There was a hook in its mouth, and the fishermen clustering around thought that it must have broken the line of an earlier fisherman. When the broken line got tangled on the pier, the poor eel had to just hang there and wait!

We took it back to our holiday house in the boot but didn't know what to do with it. We knew that some people ate eel, but that idea seemed too much to cope with. We buried my eel after we'd photographed us with it. It had begun to smell.

After dinner, we would often go for a walk up the road to the township of Ocean Grove. It would be getting dark and people would be out for a walk like us, and it seemed we all ended up at the ice cream shop. There was no guarantee that Dad would let us have an ice cream, but when he did, I loved choosing something different from Eaglehawk's choice of vanilla, strawberry or chocolate. Here you could have green or swirly ones or flavours with lumps of toffee in them. I was happy walking along the street with my ice cream, and sometimes even Mum and Dad had one.

There was also a hamburger shop up at Ocean Grove, and I longed to have my first hamburger ever. I was about seven and could easily have eaten a hamburger at any time of day or night, but Mum and Dad didn't let me have one after dinner. However, one wet day, we were allowed to have hamburgers for lunch. It was wonderful to watch the ball of meat being squashed and fried next to the onions and the bacon. The cook toasted the roll and stacked it with meat, tomato sauce, bacon, onions, then tomato, beetroot and lettuce and, finally, the rounded half roll to make a lid on top. It was wrapped in a bit of paper like fish and chip paper and then put in a paper bag. We sat in the car which steamed up as we ate and dribbled sauce and meat juice, and it was the best thing ever!

What was not the best thing ever was our holiday at Portarlington. I was nine, and Jane and Richie were seven and five. That year, there didn't seem to be a real plan for a holiday, but quite suddenly, it seemed that we were going to a place called Portarlington, where we would be camping. We never camped! We crammed into the car, packed high as usual for a holiday, but stopped outside the City Family Hotel in Bendigo. We all waited in the car while Dad and Rich went into the camping and disposals shop over the road to buy a tent. I didn't like this. It didn't seem sensible to just buy a tent on the way. The Famous Five would plan their camping holiday and talk about it in advance. Mum didn't seem very happy either. Dad must have decided the whole thing and just said that we'd do it.

After the usual endless drive, involving Geelong of course, we eventually arrived at this new place and saw the camping ground opposite the shops. It was full of tents crammed in together right up to the edge of the road. We found the turning into it and learnt from the office that there were a few places left right up at the very end. The car, the bathtub Vanguard, drove slowly past all the tents, when out of one of them, emerged one of Dad's patients. He had recognised the car and Dad, and he waved excitedly. Dad tried not to see him. 'I'm on holiday,' he growled. I was embarrassed. I knew this would be even more awful than I'd thought. Dad did not like seeing patients out of context.

We got to the end where there was some space left, and Dad drew up near a pine tree.

'That's got a branch we can tie the tent on to,' he decided. So we parked next to the tree.

'Had we better put something under the wheels?' Mum asked. It was quite a slope down towards the beach.

So, the tent came out. There didn't seem to be anything to make it stand upright, which is why Dad wanted to have it hanging from a branch. We did have some rope so I climbed up the tree and we got the tent tied up front and back from the branch. Then we tried getting it into a tent shape by pulling it out sideways but found that Dad hadn't bought tent pegs. Alright! We kids were sent off to search for some sticks or something and scavenged through the ground and down round the beach, which looked a bit boring after Ocean Grove. I found an old umbrella and a few pieces of wood. Somehow, we tied it down enough but the whole thing looked really saggy and silly. The front rose above the ground and sort of just flapped there.

During all this, the patient came up and cheerily asked if we needed any help. We obviously did, but Dad said, 'No, thank you,' and he went away. I was mortified. We looked such a shambles. I was to sleep in the tent with Mum and Dad while Rich and Jane would sleep on the front and back seats of the car. They told me much later that they had been terrified that the car would roll off into the sea. Mum and Dad had a blow up mattress, but I slept just on the ground. It was hard and not very comfortable.

During the night, the cars on the road sounded really close and their headlights flashed into the tent. I imagined their wheels rolling past, really close to my head.

Each morning, Mum dug a little hole in the ground beside the tent and was sick in it.

'Mum. What's wrong?'

'Oh, it's alright. The new baby makes me sick in the morning.'

'Oh.' I remembered that there was another baby growing in Mum but hadn't known that it made her feel sick. I felt very sorry for her.

We'd go down to the beach, which was flat and had silty sand that was not gold and crunchy like it should be. Mum would sit under our green and brown beach umbrella. I suppose we swam. On her way back to the tent one day, Jane gashed her shin really badly on someone's big, solid tent peg. Her leg bled a lot and it was horrible. She had to sit on the beach for the rest of the holiday with her leg bandaged up.

I can't remember Mum cooking or what we ate. A photo shows a small two-burner stove. I do remember water being heated, so Dad could have hot water to shave with. There's a photo of that too! Maybe we ate takeaways. It was a dismal, humiliating holiday. I look fed up and sulky in every 'happy' holiday snap!

The week or two away at the sea was more than just a break from home. It took us to a completely different world of blue sea, golden sand and freedom. Each year, I felt a mixture of recognition and discovery. I was happy to have our family together and relaxed. The repeated trips amalgamated to become a substantial part of my life. I had absorbed the Australian mythology of the beach holiday.

With my own children, to get away from the city cheaply, we camped; first with a baby and then a toddler and a baby. The camping with babies ended one wet week at Anglesea, when our toddler vomited her way through all her clothes and bedding. We packed up the wet tent, the vomitty portacot and clothes and left!

That started our run of rented holiday houses, which were a much better option with little children. We enjoyed finding the houses (pre-Google), discovering the strange kitchen utensils and saggy beds and having the comfortable easy access to the beach. It didn't matter if it rained: we were not in a tent!

When the children became older, we started loading up the car and trailer with the camping gear again and began a long run of holidays at Mallacoota. We always chose a site at the end of the camping ground on the cliffs because it had a wild and beautiful view overlooking the estuary. Our tent was good, but Mallacoota meant wind and rain and that meant tarps. I loved working out the best tarp combination for wind and rain shelter and enjoyed strolling around the camp ground checking out other people's tarps and getting ideas for improvement. I was the self-designated Queen of the Tarps and it was a far cry from the Portarlington camping fiasco.

Once set up and fully tarped, we'd sit with a coffee, gazing through the trees at the water glinting and stretching out in front of us. It would have been an eight- or nine-hour drive to escape from our dry bushland garden at Warrandyte, on the outskirts of Melbourne, and all that blue water just in front of us was worth every minute. The girls would ride their bikes around the camping ground; we'd all go up to the shops together to buy food for dinner, and we'd swim and explore the clean, wild beaches.

We now have a beach house south-east of Melbourne, an

area with beautiful beaches and quietness. The family comes and goes, and except for Christmas and Easter, it's mostly just Nick and me enjoying extended weekends. It's comfortable, familiar, surrounded by trees and birds and not a city flat. I can step out the door with a cup of coffee in my hand, eat outside, do a bit of gardening and, in winter, light the fire.

The beach holiday is still about escape, family, the sea and absence of work. A potent mix!

Chapter Nine
Taking Risks

The Eaglehawk and Bendigo landscapes held constant reminders of our gold rush beginnings. From the tram, I saw the skeletal towers of abandoned timber poppet-heads (the towers holding the winding gear for lifts down into underground mines) and huge grey sand dumps and mullock heaps lurking behind borders of pepper trees. Basalt had been blasted from the underground reefs in pursuit of the gold-bearing quartz and the mullock heaps were made of the discarded crushed basalt, 'mullock'. As the tram climbed the steep bridge crossing the railway line at Job's Gully, I looked down on little mounds of mullock amongst the scrub on the creek bed. The bush we explored was pockmarked with hollows and humps, and we'd sometimes come across a shallow dry-bottomed shaft, just there in front of us!

An abandoned mine sat on the corner of Willan and Kneebone Streets, only a couple of blocks behind us. It was smallish compared to most other mines and sat on a block as if it were a house, with a neighbour on each side.

We felt that this mine was ours. I liked it because it was complete. It had the poppet-head, the shed beside it where the gold had been extracted and the heap of mullock at the end of the trolley bridge which still stretched from the poppet-head tower. There was no fence, meaning that we could all play there. Droopy pepper trees lined the edges of the block, and a short track through them led towards the mine itself.

If I went close to the actual shaft and its dishevelled covering of planks, I could lean over and, through the jagged remnants of a platform about twenty feet down, see the distant pale, cold sheen of reflected light on black water. Rough boards lined the square walls down to the platform. I couldn't tell how deep the shaft was, but the water was a long way down. I liked to drop a piece of mullock, listen to the pause, hear the deep 'plop' and then watch the rippling shimmer. I knew it was a bit dangerous, but I always took care around the edges and never stepped onto the planks.

After that, I'd climb the poppet-head to the top. Like all the local mines, the tower was built of timber. Some timbers had been left to weather to grey, and others were painted white. Four strong posts made from tree trunks leaned in to form the little square at the top which supported the iron poppet-head wheel. There were no longer any cables. Two or three platforms, fitted between the four posts, had a square hole in the middle for the cables to run up and down as they raised and lowered the miners and brought the trolleys full of rock to the surface. Each platform was linked by a staircase. I can't remember whether the steps from the ground to the first level were still intact. Maybe I had to get to the first level and the remaining stairs by climbing up and across the trolley bridge from the top of the mullock heap. I had to be really careful on this bridge and would look for rotting boards and anything wobbly. Once on the first level, there were easy stairs to climb up the platforms until you reached the ladder-like staircase that led to the small framework at the top for the rusty poppet wheels.

Up there, I'd look around over the streets and see the bush stretching out from the edge of Eaglehawk's houses. I liked seeing the roofs from above and looking into the backyards, which were usually hidden from the street. If I looked down between the wheels and through the centre of the tower, and if the light were right, I would catch another glimpse of the sun's reflection in the water below.

The disintegrating corrugated iron shed next to the mine still housed large, rusty cyanide vats and machinery. I could see these through the gaping door, which was loosely locked by a chain and padlock, so loose that small children like me could squeeze through. I did this once. Inside, it was dark and cobwebby, lit only by dust-swirling shafts of light, and I was scared that there might be a man in there, or a snake coiled in a corner. The shed was too frightening to go into again.

The mullock heap, maybe about the height of the next-door rooftops, was the best thing to actually play on. It was solidly packed with loose sides of shifting, dark grey shattered stones and some well-worn chutes made by years of sliding children. I'd scramble up to the top, fighting the downward-sliding stones and then have a choice of how to go down. I could run, slipping and sliding with the stones, and reach the bottom, feeling triumphant for not having fallen over. Or I could sit and slide down, pushing with my hands. That wasn't much fun, really, and you could only do it on the really loose mullock. It was much better if there was a bit of corrugated iron left by some other kids. If I sat on that and pushed off, there'd be a really good slide down. The only problem then was my hands. It was hard to hold the edge of the iron because I might cut myself or my hands could get bumped on sharp stones as I shot down. I loved being settled on the sheet of iron at the top of the slope and then pushing off, trying to keep facing forward and not get bounced off, and hoping that I'd go really fast. I still remember the sound of the clashing stones as I slid and crunched across them.

Sometimes, amongst all the stones, I could find a good taw for hoppie. It would be about the size of the palm of my hand and flat on both sides. The flatness made it good for sliding accurately after I'd thrown it towards the base I wanted to hit, and also good for kicking in that particular hopscotch game. Once, I found one with a cluster of fool's gold tucked into its side. It was my best taw ever and I kept it in my blazer pocket all winter.

Sometimes, the mullock was crushed again for further gold extraction and became sand. This sand made our sand dumps.

We used to play on a sand dump at the Cal Gully Baths. Mum would have to drive us to Cal Gully (California Gully) along the main road and tram line to Bendigo, turn right at the little cluster of shops and park under the willows and pepper trees at the baths. It was only a couple of miles but out of my neighbourhood, so I didn't feel like going there by myself on my bike. The baths were scooped out at the edge of a huge collection of sand dumps. There was a bubby pool, like ours at Eaglehawk, fenced off at the end near the car park, and up at the deep end was a narrow timber deck crossing from side to side. This had a three-metre white wooden diving tower rising from the centre with the usual one-metre diving board beside it. That tower was the first three-metre board I knew, and it was a good place to pluck up the courage to jump off. These baths weren't usually crowded.

There was a concrete edge to the baths, and the surrounds were just flat, hard sand. We could do big run-ups and jump out into deep water.

Sometimes we'd leave the water and run across the baking sand to the sand dump, about a hundred yards or more away, doing the running-on-hot-sand-in-bare-feet run. The slope of soft sand here was bigger than our usual Victoria Street dune. We could do terrific jumps and slides, then run all the way back to the cool water, hurl ourselves in and wash the sand out of our bathers and hair.

Sometimes, Mum would bring us here even in winter and we would jump and jump.

After one of these Cal Gully jumping afternoons, she said something to me like, 'I worry about what you're doing to your insides with all this jumping.'

'What do you mean?'

'Oh, whether you'll be alright for having babies.'

What! I was no more than nine. I was not the least bit interested in babies. I felt sure my insides were capable of holding themselves together and not getting loose. I already knew that boys had a lot more fun than girls, and this added to the unfairness. She wasn't worried about my brother's insides.

I was so indignant about this that, as soon as we got home, I told Dad and asked him the question. He said that he thought my insides would probably be alright and went back out to the garden, leaving me still annoyed with Mum, having to think about insides and babies.

It didn't stop me jumping. There was a really good sand dump at the top of Victoria Street, over the railway line. We'd only go there in groups as it was isolated and the sort of place you needed company for. There might be a group of kids playing around on their bikes in Church Street, when someone would say, 'Let's go to the sand dumps.'

'Yeah. Let's go!'

And we'd be off. Racing down Church Street, turning round the pepper tree house on the corner, past Miss Cook's, then up into Victoria Street, across the main road with its tram lines and on up Victoria Street till the houses started petering out and the empty scrubby blocks appeared. Behind the big old pepper trees on the right was the sand dump. We'd bump across the track leading in, sometimes past a dumped car, until the grey walls rose beside us on our left.

We'd leave our bikes in a heap near the trees and run along a track to where we could climb onto the top of the dump. The sand was packed tightly enough for the walls to be fairly vertical and hard to the touch, and here they were too steep and slippery to climb. In places, the rain had cut narrow, steep gullies, which sometimes widened into V-shaped caves at ground level. They were interesting to look into. It would have been a lot of fun to play in there, but according to children's play lore, such caves were dangerous and could fall in on us. Plus, I'd read enough Enid Blyton adventures, school readers and comics to be aware of the inherent danger of a cave-in, so I never did more than quickly step in, feel the cold and smell the strong damp sand, before getting out and back into the sun.

Further along, this wall of solid sand became a loose slope that we climbed, slipping and pushing, up to the top of the dump, which was a huge area about the size of a footie ground. It stretched out flat, grey and gleaming with occasional eroded fissures streaking across the surface towards the edge. Near the dune-like slope were a couple of edges where the hard flat top dropped off about four feet above the soft sliding sand. We ran up and launched ourselves into the air to land in the soft sand. We hurtled into the air in pairs holding hands, and then threes, until it got too tangled. Or we did 'Records' and tried to out-leap our previous jumps. I enjoyed varying my landing style. I would either land and keep control so that I just sat and went no further, or I would perform an extravagant landing where I tumbled on and tried to keep rolling for as long as the sand would carry me.

I loved this place until one day a man appeared on the track near the pepper trees at the bottom of our dune.

I had landed from a flying leap and was sitting with my legs spread out on the cool, loose sand. He looked up at us. I rolled over and ran and slithered back up to the top.

'There's a man,' I announced. We all sort of groaned a bit but went on playing.

Next jump, I was going to try running in the air, but as I took off, I saw the man starting to climb up towards us. His old suit jacket flapped around as he floundered up the loose sand. I didn't like the look of him, even though he was quite small. His trousers were loose and floppy; he wore a grey hat and had a smoke in his mouth. He scrambled closer after I'd landed, but I climbed up and jumped again. This time, he was sitting near my landing spot. He looked at me and said something about playing. I didn't quite hear. I was embarrassed and scrambled back up to the top and jumped again. He moved even closer while I was in the air, and when I'd landed, he rolled across on to his side right next to me. I moved away again and raced up to the top.

I wanted to go on jumping, but the man had spoilt the fun. I couldn't see the landing place until I took off, and I wanted to go on landing in that place. It was the best because it had the deepest sand to slide in. I ran and jumped again. He rolled across and put his leg across my legs. I looked at my smooth brown legs covered by his dirty trousers. His face was close, and I saw his hard, wrinkly brown skin. His smile was full of dirty brown–grey teeth. I was confused by this and didn't like it, so I moved away and climbed back up to the top. My brother and sister looked at me, but I couldn't stop jumping. I was sort of out of control in this strange contest between the tramp and me.

Next jump, he rolled even further on to me.

'Do you like wrestling?' he said.

He tried to make it a rolling and wrestling game. That broke the spell. I liked wrestling with my playmates, but this felt horrible and peculiar. Why did he want to play with me? Why didn't he play with the others? I pushed away and ran up to the other kids.

'Let's go home!'

We ran and slid down past him to the track and started walking to our bikes.

The man appeared beside me.

'Where are you going? Can I come?' He kept on trying to talk to me. I felt awkward and didn't know what to say or do.

I kept walking. Somehow, he'd cut me off from the others, who were now ahead of us and around the corner. It didn't seem possible to just abruptly run away from him.

'In here!'

He suddenly pushed me sideways through a long hanging veil of pepper tree fronds into the tree cave inside.

'Get down!'

He pushed me over and lay right on top of me. The green leaves were all around me, and his brown face and grey clothes were all over me. He wriggled and pushed his hips up and down against mine.

'NO!' I yelled. 'Get off!'

I heaved and pushed and yelled with all my strength and got out from under him. I burst through the green wall and ran up to the others. They were still picking up their bikes and messing around. I looked back. The man was not there. I didn't say anything.

I rode home really fast. Inside, I just sat by myself on the couch in the dining room and felt very strange. Mum was doing something in the kitchen, but I couldn't see her. Dad was playing the piano in the drawing room. I felt bad and scared and guilty and confused. Suddenly, I remembered babies and penises. What would happen to me? I now knew it had all been about his penis, but he did have his clothes on. I was scared. I had to ask. I sat there and shouted into the kitchen.

'Mum! Will I have a baby if a man lies on me?'

She appeared at the door between the two rooms.

'Oh! No.' She paused to think. 'You're too young. Why?'

'A man lay on me up at the sand dump.'

She turned away to find Dad. I sat there by myself. When they were both there, I told them about the man.

'I should ring the police,' Dad said, and he went to the phone.

Mum went back to the kitchen. I sat there, still by myself, on the couch. It was good to hear his voice coming from the back room where the phone was. He came in and told me that the police would go and look for the man. Then, he went back to his piano, leaving me sitting there by myself.

I went and read on my bed. I was still disturbed. A bit later, the phone rang. I heard Dad answer, and after he hung up, he said something to Mum. I heard her footsteps coming down the hall to the bedroom. She told me that the police had gone to the sand dump but couldn't find the man. The policeman had said the tramp would be well on the move by now. That seemed to be good news.

As an adult and parent, I look at that little girl sitting alone in the middle of the couch and still find it hard to believe the minimal reaction from my parents to a sexual assault on their daughter. I was not given a single cuddle. I was given no help in how I might avoid that situation another time, and it was never mentioned again. It was as if it had never happened.

But it had, and I had made a bad choice in not leaving the sand dump earlier, when he first started getting too close. If he'd been a big man, I think I would have felt threatened much sooner. As it was, I had been able to fight back and escape.

I was surprised and a bit pleased that Dad had made that phone call. Surprised because he usually didn't seem to notice me, and pleased that he had bothered to do something about it.

Throughout my childhood, I wanted him to pay attention to me, read me a story, play a game or ask me about what I'd been doing. It felt as if I weren't there in his world, and I would try really hard to get him to notice me. In the years of sitting opposite him at dinner, I would try to see if he were in a mood to talk. Sometimes he'd respond and we could talk and laugh together. I would try to follow his train of thought, which wasn't always easy as he would make unusual connections and comments. At the same time, it always felt a bit dangerous because I never knew when he'd suddenly change mood and abruptly stop talking or lose his temper. He could be verbally vicious.

One dinner time, I was happily laughing and talking with him, fizzing with excitement and led on by his giggles when suddenly, it all went wrong. I didn't see it coming.

'Elizabeth! Go to the bathroom! Go and wait for me.' He was very angry.

I was frightened. *Why the bathroom?*

I went off into the bathroom, shut the door and waited while they finished their dinner. Finally, I heard his footsteps in the hall. He opened the door, took me by the arm and sat on the chair. He pulled me across his lap and started to smack my bottom.

It felt really strange. I was about six and felt too big to be draped across his legs. The smacks didn't hurt. It felt clumsy. He stopped and left the room, closing the door.

What do I do now? I stood around in there for a while and then went back to the family, who were doing the dishes. Dad was outside. Mum didn't say anything about it to me.

This 'being sent to the bathroom' happened a few more times. I would get overexcited and cheeky in the verbal games with Dad, and I didn't seem to realise that I was running a risk until it was too late.

He would lose his temper without warning, and again I'd have to leave the table and go off to the bathroom to wait. He didn't smack me after that first time but, instead, took off his belt, held one of my arms and tried to strap my legs or any bit of me he could connect with. It didn't usually hurt much, but I felt humiliated and confused and still didn't know what to do when he left. Sometimes, I would pile all the towels into the bath and lie in there, like being in a little bed, until it felt safe to come out. Mum never said anything, either at the table or afterwards. Rich and Jane didn't know that I was being belted, and I can see that she would have tried to hide it from them. I don't think she knew how to deal with what was happening as she may have been afraid to stand up to Dad.

Again, one dinner time, I crossed an invisible line.

'Go to the bathroom!'

I did, and waited. But this time I was angry.

He came in the door trying to pull his belt out of the belt loops on his trousers. I stepped back and faced him as he stood there tugging at his belt.

'You can't even get your belt off! You can't even give me a proper belting!' I yelled. My nine-year-old scorn was immense, powerful and loud.

'Don't you dare speak to me like that.' He tried to grab me, but I jumped around in front of him towards the open door, pushed past and ran outside to my cubby.

I sat there shaking and scared that he would come out after me. I waited and waited, listening for him to walk around the side of the garage towards me. It became dark, and he still didn't come. Everything was quiet. I crept inside and past the dining room, where they all were, and put myself to bed with my big golden teddy, who usually sat on a chair in the bedroom. Soon, the dining room door opened, and Mum came up the hall with my brother and sister to put them to bed. I pretended to be asleep, hoping she would comfort me but afraid to ask. I think she stood by my bed before turning the light off. I sniffed Teddy's smell and felt his soft fur and hugged his strong round body.

That was the last time Dad sent me to the bathroom.

Throughout my childhood, this smacking and grabbing of my arm to belt me was the only physical contact my father had with me. He never hit me in rage, which might have been more understandable to me, both as a child and an adult. I wonder if he had learnt by experience that a delayed belting in the bathroom was the way to discipline a child. Certainly, corporal punishment was common in schools and hidden in quite a few households at that time.

He didn't belt the other children, and by my mid-teens, he'd become less angry and unpredictable. As far as I was concerned, the household felt calmer.

Risk-taking within the house continued with an exploration of Dad's bottle of ether. One day when he was out, Richie and I snuck into the surgery to see what it smelt like. The brown bottle sat on a shelf, reminding me a bit of the bottles in *Alice in Wonderland*. At least this bottle didn't say 'Drink Me', but it was asking to be opened and sniffed. It was a bit scary, but I opened it, raised it to my nose and took a small sniff. Bang! A black ice-cold blow thudded into my brain. I was frightened. Richie tried it and was also startled. We put the bottle back, snuck out and didn't go near it again.

By comparison, a bit of climbing seemed positively wholesome! The Buffaloes had pulled down the old stables and built a long lean-to building against the side wall of the hall. They had tidied up the yard and, on the back, built a kitchen that peered even closer over our back fence. Mum and Dad weren't too pleased about that, but it just sort of happened.

However, the lean-to was just what we kids needed. I found that we could climb up on to its flat roof and, from there, climb onto the main pointy roof of the Buffaloes. The roof wasn't painted and had weathered to the same silvery grey of the many shed roofs we could see from there. Once up, I discovered a secret, safe hidey place tucked behind the wall of the tall facade and its short return wall. Here, we could hide from both Haggar Street and our house, sit and bask in the sun on a winter's day and, best of all, climb up the slope to the ridge of the roof, turn round and slide down to be caught safely by the side wall.

It was often just me up there. Jane didn't like the climb, and I think at the start, Richard was too young to be able to do it. It was a long way up, and you could see over a lot of Eaglehawk. St Peter's up at the main road looked even bigger looming over all the houses between us. I could see the croquet lawn of the house next door. I had hoped that our neighbours would ask me in to play croquet, but they never did. Sometimes we would hear the wooden clonk of the mallet on the ball, and I would peep at the lawn through narrow cracks in the tall wooden fence between us and be envious of the formality of its smooth greenness and the mysterious little white hoops, just like the croquet club down at the park.

I liked to take things up on the roof to inhabit our secret place. Chalk was good. Eaglehawk had a lot of chalky rocks lying around on the ground, and we used them to draw with on any bit of concrete or wall we were allowed to. It was a good secret to write and draw on the back wall of the façade. Sometimes, I'd take up little things like cars or a tennis ball to roll down the corrugated iron channels.

I started to extend my repertoire of activities by sitting astride the ridge and bumping along to the end overlooking our garden. I could then climb down on to their kitchen roof, walk back to the lean-to and climb and drop down to the ground. From doing that, it was a natural progression to stand astride the roof ridge. That felt fine. I could see even further. So I stepped out, feet on the flashing laid each side of the ridge. This was a bit of a waddle and I felt I could always just sit down if I needed to. It was pretty exciting to walk along the whole length.

Well, by then, I had bottom-bumped and duck-waddled along the roof.

The next thing was to walk on the narrowly rounded ridge like a tight rope. I could do this in little sections within the sheltered part, but further along it felt very open and exposed.

I decided that to go beyond that, I would need to check the guttering to see if it would hold me if I lost balance and slid down the roof. I tried out the guttering on the lean-to side. It was strong enough to hold me, and I scuttled along the whole length like that, with the safety net of the lean-to beneath me. I then tested the other side, which was far worse. There, it was a sheer drop of about two storeys. I started from the front, where there was the brief shelter of the side wall of the façade. I crept out over the drop. Each side step, I pushed at the guttering to test it, but I was too scared to go far. It was too dangerous. Back in the sheltered corner, I decided that the best plan was not to overbalance at all, and if I did, I'd aim myself towards the lean-to. 'Hmm,' says the adult observer!

So, there I was, standing upright, both feet on the ridge, arms out for balance. I took a step forward, then another and another. I kept moving, maintaining the momentum, looking intently at the ridge ahead of my feet. I daren't stop for a moment, nor dare to think, nor shift my gaze until the tightrope walk ended. I stepped astride the ridge and stood safely in the late afternoon sun.

There was our back garden below my feet: the fruit trees along the back fence, the clothes line full of clothes, the chook yard to the right, the garage with its roof which I'd got bored with, the lawn and swing, the mulberry tree in the side garden and the gravel drive out to Church Street on the other side.

It was another world: in shadow, distant and empty.

That one walk was enough! I had done it but knew better than to try my luck again.

It was less dangerous to climb the beautiful pine tree down in the park. Although the lower branches had been lopped off, there was a long one which drooped down over the embankment of the lake. We could jump and bounce on it, like a horse or a see-saw. It was also possible to climb up it to the trunk.

After that, it was just a matter of climbing up, twisting and stepping and pulling my way up through the branches to the very top. Here, the branches opened and spread to make a sort of sitting platform. Once up there, I could change focus from the trunk and branches to look out over Eaglehawk through the sparse pine needles. The lake lay below me. The Whipstick forest spread for miles in a grey-green canopy of small box trees to my right past the last street. The marshy overflow area reached out to the pine plantation behind me, and I could see some houses straggling along the streets: Napier, Victoria, Church. Looking down gave a bit of a whoosh to the stomach. The other kids looked very small from up there. The climb down was harder and more frightening, especially the gap where I had to hang from one branch while my feet felt for the next one below me. Coming down felt as good an achievement as the climb up, and I was really proud of that climb.

I loved climbing. I think it was about seeing if I could do it, feeling strong and coordinated and then having the reward of being up high and looking around, all by myself.

I liked being high up but was also intrigued by a tunnel. Bendigo had 'The Creek', which was a big open sandstone channel, about ten feet deep, that held the trickle of the Bendigo Creek. It ran beside roads and houses through Kangaroo Flat and Golden Square towards the centre of Bendigo. Just before the big crossroads and the Fountain, it disappeared underground between the City Family Hotel and the Lyric Theatre before reappearing to run alongside the city edge of Rosalind Park heading towards Lake Weeroona. Come to think of it, the setup was not unlike the Eaglehawk Creek channel and tunnel, but where it emerged into the park up near the terminus, it was dark, slimy and narrow. I didn't want to go near it!

I was aware of the Bendigo Creek because, while walking or catching the tram to the Fountain from school, we could see bridges crossing it just a block away. And, of course, I knew it ran between the park and the conservatory, Post Office and law courts. It was exciting to think that the channel probably ran for about a hundred and fifty yards, three Olympic pool lengths, almost directly under the Fountain where we waited for the tram each day after school. Trams from four directions – Kangaroo Flat to Lake Weeroona, and Eaglehawk to Quarry Hill – crossed at the Fountain. So did the highways from Melbourne, Mildura, Shepparton and Echuca. This big, rambling intersection at the centre of Bendigo had a secret tunnel running beneath it.

I made a plan to walk through it. I'd do the walk one day on my way home from school, and decided that I'd have to enter the creek a couple of blocks back, before it was hidden and blocked by the buildings backing on to it. My sister and I usually walked from school to the Fountain, and on that day, I told her to go on and wait for me at the Fountain tram stop. I took the surreptitiously packed torch out of my satchel, which I then persuaded her to carry for me, and headed towards the creek. At a road bridge across the creek channel, I waited till I saw no one, slid over the stone edge and dropped on to the creek bed.

My head was below ground level, but as I'd still be visible from the bridge, I hurried off along the gently sloping stone pavement. The trickle of water ran along the pavement's central groove to my right. We curved towards the town centre, and I was hidden from street view. Now, the office and hotel buildings encroached on the creek, making a shadowy canyon. Drains carrying smelly water issued from the side walls. I hadn't expected these but it was easy enough to jump over them. There were some overlooking windows, and I hoped no one saw this girl in her Girton uniform, still wearing her beret and blazer, down in what was now clearly a drain. My eleven-year-old bravado left me, and I felt small and alone.

Now, about ten yards ahead of me, loomed the entrance to the tunnel. There was nothing special about the actual rectangular opening. It was maybe about five or six yards wide and comfortingly high. I tested the torch and stepped forward under the roof. The half-light didn't last for long, and soon the tunnel felt completely different.

The blackness was thick and nearly engulfed a tiny square of light far in the distance. It stopped me. I was frightened but still excited by the idea of walking under the road. I switched on my torch and was relieved by the small cone of yellow light. The darkness was heavy, and with the loss of daylight went the loss of background sound. I heard only my footsteps and, when I stopped walking, the faint trickle of the remnant creek on my right.

I learnt to be careful with where I shone the light and where my feet went. The water was black with shiny glints where the torchlight caught it. I moved on, occasionally stepping across a side drain. Soon the torchlight revealed a tributary drain that was bigger and deeper than those I had met before. It issued from a large brick arch, and I thought it probably came down from View Street. I scanned around with the torch to pick a taking off and landing point and did a short run up to jump across. I landed safely. It was a relief to get that over. I did not want the fright of slipping into dark smelly water and I did not want to re-appear with soggy shoes and socks, let alone a wet tunic.

The squares of light at each end seemed much the same size by now, so I would have been about halfway through and under the Fountain. I don't remember hearing the rumble of traffic. It was very quiet, very remote and quite frightening. I wondered if there were rats there, but rats didn't really bother me. I was more scared of coming across a lurking man but told myself that would be pretty unlikely, so far in. What I was worried about was slipping and falling. The walls were now dripping wet in places and that made the underfoot stones slimy. So I picked my way on towards the square of light, feeling anxious and flat.

The light grew bigger and bigger, the stones under my feet dried off, and it all began to feel easier. Finally, I switched off the torch and emerged self-consciously, as if I'd suddenly stepped through a dark curtain into the lights of centre stage, not knowing if there would be an audience. Luckily, there was no audience. The sandstone walls became warm and yellow again and the green of the big elms lining the creek stretched into the blue sky. I climbed up the iron ladder that I'd checked out beforehand, pushed through a gap in the ivy covered fence and stepped on to the wide asphalt park path as if I were just out for a stroll.

It was only a few yards to the park gates and there was the Fountain – and there was my sister, waiting with two school bags at her feet. It was good to be reunited with normality. Somehow, my beret had stayed on all the time and my shoes were clean and dry. Now it was time to go home feeling pretty pleased with myself.

I think that a lot of my physical risk-taking was about getting an idea and then seeing if I could do it. I was able to judge what I could do safely. Perhaps there was a bit of luck on my side as well. I was pushing it a bit with the bees in our front garden. A huge tecoma crept and flopped over the side fence near the small front gate. Most of the year, it was just dark green, but in spring, it grew long fat buds that opened into rich orange trumpets. We liked to pull a flower out of its calyx and suck the nectar from the little opening. We knew we had to be careful that the flower didn't have a bee in it. Just imagine sucking a bee into your mouth!

One morning, Jane, Rich and I saw squadrons of bees flying around the flowering vine. We went closer and closer until I saw a brown, trembling mass of bees attached to some sheltered stems underneath the main tumble of foliage and flowers. All the other bees were zooming around in the air looking as if they didn't know what to do. The buzzing was almost like a roar now that I was up closer.

I quietly stepped further in. I was curious about how close I could get, before the bees decided they didn't like me there. Over the years, I'd had a couple of bee stings and had felt really sorry for the bee when I'd see the little clump of bee innards attached to the end of the sting in my hand or foot. I didn't mind the hurt, it'd go, but the bee would die because it had been frightened and had to attack me.

I thought that if I went very gently towards the swarm, the bees would not be startled into a panic. So I crept forwards until I had bees flying all around my head and body. The buzzing and the flying still seemed the same as it was before.

I put my hand slowly towards the swarm, closer and closer, until my finger touched the outer layer of bees. No change. I wondered if I could put my hand in and have it covered with bees. Gently and slowly, I pushed my fingers into the soft, quivering mass. It felt safe enough; the swarming bees didn't seem to mind, and the flying bees were sounding just the same. Finally, my whole hand was covered with a mound of bees up to the wrist. It was strange and exciting to feel the bees quietly moving around my hand yet know at the same time that they could be really dangerous. It still felt alright though. I gently cupped my hand and started pulling it back, very slowly bringing a brown quivering covering of bees on it. I turned and held my bee-glove up to my brother and sister who were jumping up and down with nerves and excitement.

Now I had to put the bees back. I approached the swarm and slowly put my hand back into it to reunite the bees with their friends. This time, whilst easing my hand out in slow motion, I gently straightened my fingers and the bees left me. Carefully, I stepped back through the Tacoma away from all the buzzing and back into the world.

'Elizabeth! What are you doing?' Wowo had appeared from across the road and stood watching me alongside a patient who was on her way back out to the street.

'I'm alright. I was careful.'

I had learnt to manage myself with straight out physical risk. However, I needed help with risk of violence towards me. I needed to be told about what had happened with the man at the sand dumps, and how I might manage situations better in the future. I also needed comfort. It was hard to have to rely on just myself.

Chapter Ten
Church

In Eaglehawk, it seemed that as far as church was concerned, you either went a lot or not at all. We went a lot.

St Peter's Anglican Church stood at the top of our aptly named 'Church' Street on a big corner block, which had room for both the stark, lofty 'new' red-brick church and the original sandstone building, a wooden hall, a tennis court and net shed, an abandoned grassy netball court, palm trees and gum trees and a lot of gravel and rough grass to park on.

Small children would go to Sunday School in the white wooden hall, which had a little kitchen and wood oven at the back. We'd file in through one of the two side doors and take our places at the brown benches arranged in little squares for the separate age groups' lessons. I'd sit with a bunch of kids, all in our good clothes, and we'd be told stories from the Bible, say some prayers, sing some songs and then we'd be allowed to go home or play outside until our parents came.

One day, one of the girls said, 'Ooh, your mum's getting fat.'

'No, she's not. She's having a baby.'

'What?'

'Yes. She's growing a baby in her tummy.'

'What? You can't do that!'

'You can. And then it comes out through a special hole between her legs.'

'No! That's rude. I'm going to tell on you!'

She did, and Mum got a telling-off from the girl's mother for describing such things to a child.

When we got to secondary school age, we went into the other hall for Sunday School. This was originally a little church made of pretty yellow and grey sandstone with church-shaped windows, a pointy roofed porch and a small sort of arch rising above the roof for a couple of bells to hang from. These bells had ropes attached to them that dropped down to a closed-off landing above the back of the hall. You reached the landing and the dangling ropes by a small spiral staircase behind a usually locked door. On Sundays, the minister or one of his helpers would ring the bells at 10.30, 10.45 and 11 in the morning to let us know that church was about to start. The same thing happened in the evening for Evensong. At the front of the hall was a stage with a piano.

There we'd be, in the hall, grouped by age, having our lessons. The same sort of thing happened here as in the little hall: reading a story from the Bible, trying to think of something to say about it, some hymns with music from the piano on the stage and some prayers. Sometimes we'd muck around a bit, talking about other things, wanting to be outside. Some teachers, who were all from the congregation, were really boring, others not too bad and some, I liked a lot.

I'd be in my Sunday clothes. In winter, this was usually a tartan pleated skirt, a matching jumper and a beret. I really liked the Black Watch tartan I had one year. White socks were a change from brown school ones and made my brown lace-up shoes look brighter. In summer, I'd have a cotton dress and some Clarks' T-bar leather sandals. I loved the quietness and softness of their crêpe rubber soles. We very rarely bought a ready-made dress or skirt, and I'd enjoy choosing the material for these dresses from the shop in Bendigo. Mum made them or we'd go to a dressmaker. She'd get child endowment cheques from the government, and that was usually the signal for a set of clothes and shoes for the next season.

After Sunday School, we'd walk into the real church to sit at the front for the first bit of the communion service. This church was newer than the little stone hall and was vast – high, wide and open. The inside walls were white and decorated with a couple of painted scrolls bearing Bible quotes. Mum would be in the choir in front of us, and Dad tucked away playing the organ, which was really a harmonium. Miss Prance used to play the organ, but I think Dad took over fairly soon after arriving in Eaglehawk. Apparently, Miss Prance was glad to be able to retire. The three of us kids were arranged in our various classes in the front rows. Later, Rich became a server so was up the front with Mum and Dad.

It was always a battle for Mum to get out of the house on a Sunday morning without Richie's dog, Brutus, following her up the street. Occasionally, he'd do a Houdini from the house, run up the street, sniff and trot up the aisle to track down Mum in the choir stalls, where he'd lie happily at her feet for the rest of the service. The family of the vicar, Mr Ross, had a similar problem with their dog, Socks, who would come down a block from the railway side of the main road in search of his family. Relations between the dogs were not always harmonious. One Sunday, the dogs met in the aisle and enjoyed a brief snapping and growling altercation. One of the Ross boys grabbed Socks and took him outside. Brutus continued on his way to join Mum, and the service continued as if nothing had happened. Richie was a server that day and saw all this from in front of the altar. At times, it would be his turn to take the cross and lead the procession out of the church, including Mum, Brutus and Dad, and try to keep a straight face.

On a 'good' day, the church was full, and it was fun to sing the hymns with all those voices behind and in front of us. We learnt to listen for some of the men's roaring or droning voices and some of the trilly, wobbly ladies and try not to get the giggles. Generally, it was a strong, nice sound, and lots of the hymns had tunes and words that I liked.

On a hot summer's morning, it was an enjoyably strange experience to sing the words,

'In the bleak midwinter,

Frosty wind made moan.

Earth stood hard as iron,

Water like a stone.'

The tune was deep and melancholy, and I'd be thinking about going swimming that afternoon.

The choir sang an anthem that Dad had taught them at choir practice on Wednesday nights. The anthem was always the slightly anxious bit for me because Dad would choose new, different tunes which the choir sometimes had trouble with. Mum, who sang really nicely, would get nervous about the reception these anthems would have from the congregation. Most of them liked what they were familiar with. We'd have the lesson, yet more Bible reading, prayers, another hymn, and then the minister would give a little children's sermon to us before releasing us and getting on with the serious business of communion.

What a relief it was to walk slightly self-consciously down the aisle and run outside. We'd walk home down the street and into the unlocked house perfumed with the Sunday roast that mum would have 'put in' before going up to church. We'd change out of our good clothes and wait for mum to come home in a bit of a flurry about the roast and 'how it was'. It was always safe, and she would soon serve us up roast meat, gravy and lovely crispy roast vegetables. There was always a sweet.

Dad used to play the organ for Evensong too so would slip out of the house at about half past six. When we were a bit bigger, Mum would go to Evensong too. I never liked them both being out at night, even if it was when Pa was staying with us.

Often there'd be christenings during the service at the font on the side. However, when it was time to christen Sally, we had an afternoon service so that Nana and Da could come. Nana, wearing a grey suit, a fox wrapped around her neck and her hair immaculately waved, had to be helped into the church because she didn't walk much any more. The christening began, but Nana started crying a bit noisily so was helped outside to sit in the car. I was getting bored so I went outside too. Nana called me over from the open window of the car and leant towards me. Her bright red lipstick had smudged around her drooping mouth, and in a sort of crying talking, she said, 'Elizabeth. You must look after your mother. She has a hard life.' She was fully crying now and unable to speak.

I hated this. I knew what she meant and said something like, 'Alright,' and went off to look at the tennis court. I was a nine-year-old child. It wasn't my job to look after my mother! But somehow, I had already taken up that responsibility of my own accord. Throughout our shared lives, I continued to feel that I had to protect Mum. Despite myself, I couldn't stop doing it.

Church was part of school life too since Girton was a 'Church of England Girls' Grammar School'. We had prayers, like a little church service, each morning for about half an hour. Scripture was one of our lessons. I didn't like it, couldn't be bothered and usually got a pretty low mark.

The church's repeated teaching made me guilty about not being a kind, generous person all the time. The message from the Bible and the prayer book was that I could never be good enough and that God would always find something wrong with me. It seemed that He knew more about me than I did and was always watching me and reading my mind to gather up the bad bits about me. For Lent one year, instead of giving up lollies, I tried giving up being nasty to my sister. 'Nasty' meant teasing her, usually about some funny steps she had learnt at ballet and other girly stuff. As adults, Rich and I realised that she didn't know how to bounce back from a jokey tease, which made her even more vulnerable. In hindsight, we felt a bit bad about that. I was being a smart alec with that sacrifice, and it rebounded on me because I found it was hard to stick at, harder than giving up lollies. I couldn't wait for Easter Sunday.

I didn't like to be put in the position of having to ask to be forgiven for my sins and then have the minister say that God had forgiven me. I knew I would not murder anyone nor 'covet my neighbour's wife nor his oxen'. It seemed that God was pretty ready to punish people.

I did take notice of 'Do unto others as you would have them do unto you.' That seemed a good way to behave in the world.

What the church did do really well was to provide our family with a social life that would otherwise have been non-existent.

I remember slide nights in the little hall, where we once sat for a whole evening looking at slides of snowflakes while someone talked about them. This was pre-TV. The benches had been put in rows; the wood stove at the back was lit; the lights were turned off, and on the screen appeared large single snowflakes against a coloured background. I learnt that each snowflake was slightly different from another despite having the same basic form of six points. I loved looking at the endless stream of snowflakes shining in the dark room, but some people were getting restless. Other nights, we would have slides of people's holidays, which I didn't find anywhere near as interesting. There was also a night of camellias.

Always, there was the reward of supper. The mothers brought food; the urn came to the boil, and tea was made in a huge pot. I didn't like tea but would try a cup with heaps of sugar. I would eat a lot of food, then run around screaming in the dark in the churchyard with the other kids.

Occasionally, there were concerts in the other hall, which had the stage. People sang, played the piano, recited poems, and children did ballet. It was good to watch, but I never had any urge to get up on stage.

The adults had dances, which I didn't go to until I was about thirteen. The off-shoot for us kids was that they made the floor very slippery to dance on, and for the next few days, if we had Girls' Friendly Society Club, we could run up and down doing terrific skids.

Each year, there would be a fancy dress parade with prizes for the different age groups. Mum worked really hard to make those costumes, and her best one ever was the bee costume for Jane with lots of horizontal black-and-yellow stripes. Richard's costume one year was John Bull, like on the porridge packet. He was a sturdy little boy, and we thought he filled out his Union Jack waistcoat very appropriately.

While I still had my plaits, I went as Cinderella in my blue Sunday School dress with a white apron over it, and carried a straw broom. The exciting thing was that my hair was out of its plaits. That night, Mum had unplaited and brushed it. I didn't usually look at myself much, and it was astonishing to see all my hair so long and wavy. I quite liked it, but I was a bit nervous about appearing like that as I never went anywhere with my hair out. People did say things like 'What beautiful hair!' but I felt more self-conscious than if it had been just a costume like the bee one. The plaits went back in next day.

The sack dress arrived on the scene when I was about eleven or twelve. This sack was suddenly all over the *Women's Weekly*. Where did the waists and busts go? That year, my costume was a sack dress. Mum found a clean sack, cut out a neckline and sleeve holes, bound them with some nice material scraps that we had and added a sort of pleated frill on the bottom. I wore a hat and felt very smart.

Every social night up at the big hall ended with a full scale supper, the ladies having followed the instruction to 'please bring a plate'. Long tables covered in white cloths were placed along the side wall, and the plates would be placed on them to wait till supper time. Some food would be hidden under a napkin or tea towel, other plates under little netting umbrellas. For us kids, the nice part of the evening was to check out the food. Starting from the savoury end, I liked Savoy biscuits with butter and tomato and lots of salt and pepper, but they would get soggy if left too long. There'd be mixed sandwiches: German sausage, cheese and celery, egg mayonnaise cut into triangles. Mum would sometimes get fancy and make club sandwiches. The oven in the little hall would have heated up sausage rolls and party pies. Little Cheerios would be steaming and ready to burn your mouth. Bowls of tomato sauce lay waiting for dipping. Then you could go on to scones: plain, savoury or sweet. Then cakes: hedgehog, Chocolate Crackles and Honey Joys, cupcakes in paper wrappers with pretty icing, or with their tops cut off and halved and then poked back into the jam and cream which had been spooned on to the cut top of the cake. Finally, the real cakes! There'd be a solid fruit cake, which adults liked more than I did, orange cakes, tea cakes and, best of all, cream sponges. I loved these for their soft sweetness and their rarity.

There were cups of tea and fizzy drinks provided by the Oswalds, who had a small soft drink factory. Men went out to smoke; women worked like mad and kids would eat.

There were religious dates and events like Christmas day and Easter, which moved around in mysterious ways at the end of summer. But we had one fixed day, the first Tuesday in November which was the Sunday School picnic and incidentally, the Melbourne Cup. The day was a state-wide public holiday and really special in Bendigo because it was the day that the Sunday Schools of all the religions had their picnics.

Eaglehawk took itself off to Marong by steam train. Dad would drop Mum, us kids and the picnic down at the station early in the morning. We'd push through the crowds and find where the St Peter's crowd was waiting. The other churches were in their groups along the platform. Most trains were diesels by then, so it was exciting to travel by the picnic steam train. We were used to the blaring horn of the diesel engines but knew that the steam train would whistle as it approached the station.

'*Whooo Whooo!*' it screamed, as it puffed along behind the Eaglehawk streets.

'Here it is!'

'Come here, now! Hold my hand.'

Families clustered and shouted above the hissing and steaming of the engine pulling in front of us. The pistons and wheels slowed. We picked up our bags and baskets and got ready to rush aboard for the best seats.

'Step back! Step back!' The station master shouted and blew his whistle at the seething Sunday School crowd. The train stopped with a monstrous explosion of steam and we climbed up into the dark red carriages.

Each family would end up in a little group of wooden seats. First kid to the window would pull it down and lean out in triumph. Right! Now we could go. There would be more shrill whistle-blowing by the station master from the platform; the train's whistle screamed; the roar of the engine deepened and we felt a trembling tug as the carriages jolted in line. I loved hearing the deep *choof choof choof choof* as we gathered speed and left Eaglehawk.

We passed the golf course and entered the bush and paddocks. By now, the train was moving along faster, never as fast as we'd have liked, but if you put your head out the window, there was a lot of wind. You had to be careful to squint up your eyes as much as you could while still being able to see, because of the peril of getting soot in your eye. On each trip, at least one kid would suddenly throw himself back into the carriage shouting and crying, 'My eye! My eye.' The mum would say, 'I told you so,' spit on her hankie and try to wipe the soot out.

We'd settle a bit, but soon the mothers would start picking up baskets and saying, 'We're nearly there, I think.' Yes, there was the creek and the bridge, there was the picnic ground and oval and, a sure sign, more ear-splitting whistles as the train approached Marong station. Once there, down we climbed and jostled our way off the platform heading in a straggle along a gravel road towards the picnic ground.

It was quite a long walk with the little children and picnic baskets and rugs but eventually, we crossed the ramshackle wooden bridge over the creek and spilled into the picnic ground. It was really a big block of land with a fenced off oval in the middle, a couple of tin sheds for the Ladies and Gents, and another where you could buy the Oswalds' fizzy drinks, a water tank, the creek running alongside and lots of longish dry grass. Gum trees gave some shade. Each church seemed to know where its area was, and we'd set up for the day. It would be nice when Mum had put the brown tartan picnic rug down so we could all sit down and have a drink. One year, we got ourselves next to an old fallen tree trunk so we could sit with our backs against it and look out, feeling very comfortable. Her church friends would set up nearby, and we'd run off to explore.

From the top of the creek's dry clay banks, I looked down at dark brown water lying still. In places, bulrushes stood in the water. Fallen trees, weathered to a gleaming grey, plunged into the gully. It was hard to get down to the water because of the steep banks and the tangle of dead wood. I was scared of snakes hiding there. A bit further on, a large trunk crossed the whole creek. I could walk across it and follow the creek bed down along the other side. Each year, it was still much the same and a bit hard to know what to do in such a prickly, unfriendly place. There was nowhere to paddle because the banks dropped off so steeply. All you could do was throw sticks into the water and see if they moved.

However, there was always lunch. I knew Mum would have made a bacon and egg pie, which I loved, especially as we only had it at the Sunday School picnic. The day before, Gladys would make pastry, and Mum lined a big flat baking dish with it.

Then she broke in a lot of eggs and laid rashers of bacon on top. When it came out of the oven, the pastry was golden and the eggs and bacon were cooked solid.

I went back to the rug and there was lunch set out. Mum cut out the first slice of the pie, which always made her a bit nervous and she'd talk about whether it would have 'worked'. I liked seeing the pie slice side-on. There was a solid yellow bit of yolk, some egg white, the pinky-brown strips of bacon and the darker brown pastry. It tasted so good, and we all agreed that it was perfect food for a picnic and easy to carry on the train.

Once or twice, Dad drove out to have lunch with us and watch the races. Usually, he stayed home and I guess had a nice quiet day to himself!

After lunch, we had to wait for the races to start. These were held on the bit of smooth dirt track that ran around the edge of the grassy bit of the oval. There were running races for the different age groups. I'd go in these but never enjoyed them much because basically, I was just not a good runner. What I did like were the novelty events.

There were egg and spoon races where we put a dessert spoon in our mouth, were handed an egg to place in the spoon and then ran a race trying to keep the egg from falling. That created a lot of very funny walky-runs. The sack race was fun. You had to climb into a sack, and over the years, I worked out that it was a good idea to push my toes into the corners to keep the sack from flopping about and tripping you up. Then the choice was between doing a lot of little fast steps on your toes or making giant jumps. Seeing we did this only once a year, I never did find the better technique. The three-legged race was best if you could find a partner much your size so that when we tied our legs together we had a good chance of being able to run quite smoothly.

There was a fathers' race, which got pretty competitive. The men took off their jackets and lined up with a lot of jostling and joking. Some looked as if they were trying not to look as if they were really keen. I liked seeing the men run really fast and so powerfully that you could hear their feet thudding on the ground. You could really see the difference between men and boys in those races. The mothers didn't have a running race. Their race was called 'stepping the chain'. We learnt fairly early that this wasn't a metal chain but the name of a distance, twenty-two yards. The mothers would line up and then when the whistle blew, start walking along very seriously, counting their steps. Most folded their arms across their chests and looked to the ground as they paced out their measure. Each mother stopped when she thought she had paced out the distance. Then the excitement and barracking grew as the actual measurement was made. I would have loved Mum to have won that race.

The afternoon trailed away after the races, and soon it'd be time to pack up and start trickling back to the station. There was less excitement about everything on the way home. People sat back against their seats and compared sunburns. Dad would meet us at the station and drive us home.

One of the church clubs was GFS, Girls' Friendly Society, which I started going to when I was about eight. I liked walking up to the hall by myself after dinner on a week night and meeting my church friends, and racing around until the leader started the evening's programme. We played games, said some prayers and sang some songs until it was time to run home down the dark street.

One night, they read out an announcement about a GFS camp to be held at a place at the beach. I really wanted to go and asked and asked until Mum said yes. When the day came, in the early morning, Mum took me and the little suitcase which she had packed for me into the Bendigo Station to catch the seven o'clock train to Melbourne. There were a whole lot of girls from Bendigo GFS clubs but no one else from St Peter's. I was one of the youngest ones there but didn't mind that. I was going to a camp.

At the camp, we were taken to little huts amongst the tea tree, where we slept in bunks. Each cabin had a grown-up to look after us and make sure we went to bed and got up in time for breakfast. Our lady was a bit grumpy with me. I think she thought I was too little and would be a nuisance. I wasn't. I was good at getting ready for bed and getting dressed and making my bunk tidy. The only problem was my plaits which I couldn't do by myself.

'Oh! I've got to do your plaits, do I?'

'Yes, please. I can brush my hair but can't plait it.'

Each morning, she'd tug away impatiently making a pair of rather lumpy plaits while I sat there feeling a nuisance. Mum always did it smoothly and evenly.

But the rest of the time was terrific. We had a lot of food and sat in a hall to eat it. We played games and often went to the beach which was just on the other side of the band of tea tree. It wasn't summer but still good to play in the sand, building giant castles and having races. One of the helpers was a big friendly teenage girl called Kim, who had long blonde hair and was very pretty. I liked it when I ended up doing something in her group. I thought 'Kim' was the best name ever as it was one of those that could be a name for a boy or a girl. I loved being at that camp by myself.

It was only as an adult that I discovered that the camp had been at Point Lonsdale, where we went to Merrilands Guest

House a few years later. It would have been interesting to have gone and looked at the camp. Maybe Mum and Dad didn't realise that my camp had been there.

I kept going to church all through school and tried to be a good Christian. However, once I got to Melbourne University and away from the context of home, all that religion and churchgoing fell away. I found it useful to have a background of the Bible and prayer book because it was surprising how many religious references appeared in the texts I studied for English. The Church-induced guilt lasted longer. On the positive side, I still try to treat others as I'd like them to treat me. However, I think I'd have worked out that message for myself anyway.

Chapter Eleven
Guilt and Shame

There were times when both my common sense and sense of what was morally right let me down.

I really mucked it up one afternoon when we were hanging out on our bikes under the pepper trees at the corner. We were just sort of riding and playing chicken, when a group of boys pedalled up to us from around the corner. They knew the kids in our group from their school, Eaglehawk State. I didn't know them but they joined in our chicken game, which suddenly got a lot faster and closer and scarier than how we normally played it. Before we knew what had happened, the two groups started jostling and giving cheek to each other. Somehow it got to 'D'ya wanna fight?'

Apparently we did, because the whole bunch of kids gathered up and raced down the road to the park to have this fight. I went along because I was there and I wanted to see what would happen. We ended up on the tennis court next to the croquet club and surged our way past the little white weatherboard clubhouse under the oak tree, to the back court, which was a bit less open to the road. There we formed a seething clump with lots of shouting boys. I'm not sure how many, if any, girls were there.

I'm also not sure how it happened, but I found myself in the centre of what was now a ring of kids, facing up to a boy I'd never seen before. I liked wrestling but had never had a fight with fists. It felt a bit peculiar to be doing this, but I thought I'd give it a try.

The boy and I stood looking at each other. He was a little bit shorter than I was and was bouncing on the spot with his fists up, doing little punches in the air. I decided to put my fists up too but felt it looked a bit silly doing the bouncing, so didn't. The boy bounced towards me and suddenly there he was, quite close. He shot his arm out and punched me on the left shoulder. That hurt! He had a hard bony fist. So I had a go at punching him. Ouch! That hurt my fist. He hit me again.

I decided that I didn't like this and stepped back and said, 'I'm going to stop now.' I walked back through the shouting kids, picked up my bike and rode home feeling disturbed and guilty. It was a relief to turn into the drive and put my bike into the garage. I didn't want to go inside and went up to the cubby to hide. I felt that I had done something really bad but didn't really know what it was. I sat in the cubby, fidgeting around, wondering what to do.

Footsteps crunched up the drive and a big knock on the back door was followed by men's voices. Then Mum called, 'Elizabeth,' in her high lady's voice. That was scary. I walked out round the side of the garage, and there were two huge policemen standing on the gravel. I was so small against them that it seemed my head was barely higher than their belts.

They looked down at me.

'We've had reports of kids fighting down on the tennis courts. Were you there?'

I looked up at them with wide-open, honest, lying eyes and said, 'No.'

I was so frightened that the lie just came out. Might I have to go up to the Police Station in the police car? Might they put me in the lock-up with the drunks?

'Are you sure? One of the neighbours down there said that he saw the Trembath girl.'

'No, it wasn't me.'

There was some to and fro of adult talk. Dad might have come out by then. Then they left. I knew they knew it was me fighting. The tennis court neighbour was quite right about who the girl with blond hair in two plaits was. No one else in Eaglehawk had hair like that and I felt that everyone knew me.

'I'm going inside.'

I went to lie on my bed and read. I kept waiting for Mum or Dad to come and tell me off but they didn't. Dinner time came but still nothing was said. Ever.

I've thought about my readiness to lie so brazenly to the police. I had thought of myself as someone who didn't lie. I thought the truth was important. I would have told the story to Mum if it had arisen. I'd have felt a bit silly and guilty. I knew that she would really disapprove of her daughter fighting in public with a gang of boys. She would probably have done the 'I'm disappointed in you' thing with a cold, blank look on her face, which I hated because I never knew what it really meant. Did it mean she would stop loving me? Or did she love me less now? Not that the word 'love' was ever said aloud. Could I regain ground in the 'being-good stakes'? If so, how? Did I have to be good at everything, all the time?

I think it's because two huge policemen came right into my territory that I felt so threatened and instinctively defended myself. I felt ganged up on by strange adults and actually didn't care enough about them personally to tell the truth to them. It was more important to send them away. I knew that I hadn't done anything very bad, really. I was too frightened about the police and the lock-up to tell the truth.

A couple of years later, I had another very public fight. This time, it was with my best friend, who lived in the next street. We were on our way down to the park, and I have no idea why we had started fighting. It was the first time that I had ever felt angry and hurt enough by a friend to lose my temper. We started yelling at each other.

I picked up a lump of dirt from the little garden built into the brick fence of the house we were near and threw it at her. The yelling hadn't seemed enough, which is why I started throwing dirt. She looked shocked at being hit by a clod of soil and found some in the same garden to throw back at me. We continued to yell and throw dirt at each other. We were now crying through our shouting and throwing. I didn't know how to stop.

A car drove by slowly, with the window down, and a woman looked closely at us. We continued to yell. My friend started to run home, and I turned and ran home too, the long way round. By the time I got inside, Mum already seemed to know about it. Maybe some phone calls had gone round the neighbourhood. She didn't say anything.

Anyway, we started hanging around together again quite soon.

Those two fights were two very different kinds of events. In the punching fight, I was in control of myself and found it easy to stop when I wanted. I found it interesting, really. However, the fight with my friend was different in that I was feeling hurt and angry and fought with anger and loss of control.

In each case, my parents knew about the fight but didn't talk to me about it. I would have liked to be able to talk about what had happened.

I not only lied about fighting but also about carrots.

Up the road was a vegetable garden that I could see from the road. The house was on a corner block, facing the cross street, so the backyard ran along our street. I didn't really know the people in that house. They had no children and we never saw them.

Their carrots were growing very well. I watched them over the weeks as the feathery tops grew greener and greener and bigger and bushier. I loved baby carrots, but we never grew any and only bought the big, solid ones that you peel and slice for boiled vegetables or a stew.

I realised one day that the house seemed very quiet. The next day it was the same. The occupants must have been away. I climbed over the fence, pulled up a carrot, washed it under the tap and ate it. Scrumptious. Then another. And a few more. I threw the tops under the hedge. *Hmm.* This wasn't good. Someone might see me. *I'd better stop and go home.*

However, I went back the next day and ate some more, feeling even guiltier and more furtive. I didn't go back after that because the bare patch of ground where I'd pulled up the carrots was getting too big to go unnoticed.

A while later, Mum told me that the man had come back from holidays and found a lot of his carrots missing. A neighbour had seen me in the garden, he told her. Had I taken the carrots?

Again, in a flash, a denial!

'No. It wasn't me.'

This time, I lied because I was ashamed of myself for eating those carrots he had been growing so carefully. It was stealing and an unkind thing to do. I didn't want people to see me that way.

I had learnt that all you had to do was to look truthful and plainly deny an accusation to get away with it. However, I was also learning that I didn't like the way that left me feeling. I was starting to realise that it wasn't a good idea to do things I'd be ashamed of later.

Around that time, Mum and I were busy in the kitchen one day when she said in a secretive sort of voice, 'You know, Beverley told me today that someone said to her, "That Trembath girl is going to come to no good".'

'What!'

I was offended and hurt.

'Come to no good!'

Why did she say that? I know I played on the street a lot and played footie with the boys and rode around on my bike with them, and I shouldn't have stolen the carrots, but that prediction seemed way off the mark. I knew that I wasn't a gentle, girly girl, but I had no intention of 'coming to no good'. I was a clever girl and was going to get a good job and look after myself and not end up in Eaglehawk all my life.

I don't know why Mum's friend told her or why Mum told me. I didn't want to know that people were saying bad things about me. However, by then, I had taught myself another defence mechanism. I was learning to turn what had hurt me into a joke. Laughing made me feel better.

'That Trembath girl will come to no good!' became a bit of a running joke between Mum and me. I loved repeating the self-righteous, condemning words and feeling triumphant whenever I had achieved something like being top of the class or winning another swimming medal. I still enjoy saying it on occasion!

Chapter Twelve
The World Comes to Eaglehawk

It was easy to believe that our world was encompassed by the boundaries of Eaglehawk and Bendigo. I knew that there was a big town called Melbourne one hundred miles away to the south, but after my first stay with Doff and George when Richard was born, we only went to Melbourne a couple of times, and that was to visit them.

As an older child on family visits, this was an exciting place. We'd drive for a long time down the Calder Highway and then through street after street full of cars and houses and shops. Mum and Dad, outside their locality, were anxious about finding their way, and I'd be relieved when we got there. By then, I was old enough to notice and remember the tall, blocky, dirty yellow building. Once inside, the vast open space was filled with machinery on the floor; huge pipes climbed high, and everything hummed and vibrated, filling the air with almost tangible energy. A sort of footpath took you around the edge of the shiny machines and pipes to another little door in the side, which opened to a flight of metal stairs climbing up to the house. The metal staircase rose almost higher than we could imagine, and our feet made it ring and clang. I would dare myself to look down and see through the metal mesh to the receding floor. The shimmering, enveloping sound followed us all the way up and only ceased when we stepped through another door on to a wooden deck leading to George and Doff's front door.

The house sat on a platform built across the shallow ridge of the roof. Little steps led down to the coarsely asphalted sloping rooftop that surrounded the house like a garden normally would. A cream-painted concrete wall ran all around the edge of the roof like a fence, but I could only see over it at the middle of each end where the ridge sloped up to the top of the wall. Jane, Richie and I could run round and round the house, always on a slope and up and down the little bridge steps. Once, I tripped and ended up with a deep bleeding graze on my knee.

One visit, I was tired of being indoors with the adults and decided to go outside to explore. I walked across the sloping rooftop to the shallow bit of the parapet at the peak of the ridge where I could lean over and look down. I was thinking about the rubbish bins and the shopping and what fun it would be to ride down like the bins. Suddenly, there was a huge noise of shouting and running feet. I turned around. George, suit coat flapping behind his elbows, was running hard towards me. A string of adults trailed behind. They thought I might fall off the edge. I thought that was pretty silly of them. I was just looking and having a think – until I got a fright with all that shouting and running. I had to go back inside.

George was the chief electrical engineer, which was why they lived in the house on the roof. I learnt to be sorry for Doff, who apparently had something wrong with her heart so that she couldn't go down and up the stairs and had to stay in the house all the time. She was like a prisoner up there.

I loved going through the maze of humming pipes up to that place in sky. It was an adventure, like climbing into a land at the top of Enid Blyton's 'Magic Faraway Tree'.

Nowadays, I see the building quite often from the M1 freeway. The flat is clearly unused, and the roof bristles with satellite dishes.

I knew from my reading that there was a wider world than mine, but it was an English world of talking animals, adventurous children and running rivers.

Nearly everyone in Eaglehawk had been born in Australia and spoke 'Australian'. We were generally fair-haired and fair-skinned. The Eliades up at the fish and chip shop were the big exception. I knew that they came from Greece, and that was why they spoke English differently from us. We loved their fish and chips. Sometimes, I took up a bundle of *The Age* and *Bendigo Advertiser*, which I'd opened up flat for them to wrap the fish and chips in. If I was lucky, they'd give me threepence or sixpence, which I'd then take down to the milk bar to buy lollies. Sometimes, during the school holidays, other kids had got entrepreneurial before me and my roll of paper was not needed. I'd have to walk back home with my bundle under my arm.

At school, we were all Anglo-Saxon type girls until one day, a new girl appeared in the middle of the term. She had a foreign-sounding surname, long, wavy dark hair tied back, and she didn't speak much. That first lunchtime, we all went out to sit in a row against the wall of Miss Cure's classroom under the front verandah. I opened my brown paper bag and was unwrapping my cheese sandwich from its greaseproof paper when I heard sniggering from down the row. I looked up and saw June, the new girl, unwrapping a crumpled newspaper parcel. Inside was a big loose sandwich made from thick untidy slices of what was definitely not a square sliced loaf. The filling was dark brown and could have been just Vegemite.

'Oooh, look! Her lunch is in newspaper!' Giggle, giggle.

I didn't like hearing this but didn't know what to do, so I ate my sandwich and said nothing. One day, I noticed that she wasn't there any more. I think now that her family may have been Jewish refugees, and I hope that she was treated better at her next school.

Generally, in the 1950s, there were very few European migrants who had made it as far inland as Bendigo. By contrast, the Chinese had been in Bendigo since the 1850s gold rushes and were now both incorporated in our community and set apart from it. We loved the difference when it showed itself magnificently at the Bendigo Easter Fair. This fair, now called the Bendigo Easter Festival and once sponsored by a chicken farm, has been running continuously since 1871, when it was inaugurated to raise funds for the Sandhurst Benevolent Asylum and Hospital. It was so successful that in 1892 the Chinese community provided a dragon, Loong, and the Chinese part of the Easter celebration has been exciting and important ever since.

At Easter, there was a big advantage in having grandparents living at the bank. The Easter Fair had two daytime processions through the streets and a torchlight one which we rarely got to see. The Easter Saturday procession was smaller than the big one celebrating Loong the dragon on Easter Monday, but the joy of the Saturday one was that it passed right under the windows of the bank before turning into Pall Mall. The Saturday procession ended with the sea lions, dancing and prancing to the Chinese drums and getting ready to wake up the dragon on Sunday afternoon.

We would come in from Eaglehawk and get ready at the windows. The best window was wide and rumbled open high enough for us children to sit on the sill and watch and wait; my grandparents even found cushions for us. In the distance, we could hear the brass bands and the Scotchies. It took ages for the procession to arrive in the street beneath us.

'They're coming!'

First, there were the boring open-topped cars with the mayor and his good lady wife and other important people whom we didn't know. Brass bands followed, the men marching while they played. How could they play and walk at the same time? The band leader strutted and twirled his decorated rod and the huge drums rested on the drummers' stomachs. We would give a special cheer to the Eaglehawk Band in its navy blue uniforms and would look hard to see if we could recognise anyone under his peaked cap. In between the bands came the decorated floats. The formula was to have an open deck truck covered in hundreds of crepe paper flowers and people, mostly women, dressed up in some sort of fancy dress on the back. They wore a lot of makeup and waved at us. I especially liked it when the Scotchies and their bag pipes approached. They were strange and exciting in their kilts, special long white socks, black jackets and fancy berets. Even stranger and more exciting was the sound made by their bagpipes. And they, too, did this whilst marching.

At last, the brass bands and bagpipes gave way to heavy drumming. The sea lions were coming down the hill. Their heads were huge, brightly ornate and grimacing. They leapt and plunged across the street, sometimes surging towards the crowds. We saw legs in shiny, bright-coloured trousers under the head. A short train of decorated silk came from the back of the sea lions' head and was held by a Chinese man who danced and waved the tail following the lead of the dancer in the head. Drummers in Chinese costume danced and provoked the lions. The grown-ups told us that the head was so heavy that the dancer beneath had to hand over to another man after a very short time.

On Saturday, the sea lions marked the end of the procession. The crowd filled in behind and enjoyed walking down the centre of the road towards the sideshows and stalls set up around the streets. We climbed in from the window, excited and happy and looking forward to Monday's procession, which would be bigger and end with not only the sea lions but Loong himself. For that, we would have to stand in the street because the procession followed a different route. It was exciting to be part of the crowd and be close to all the bands and floats and dragons.

If we were really lucky, Mum would take us to 'The Awakening of the Dragon' on Sunday afternoon. You had to stand around in the street under the autumn elms in front of Loong's dusty weatherboard house down in Chinatown and wait for ages until the drumming started. The sea lions would jump out amongst us, dancing and dancing faster and faster. Crackers exploded and we all screamed. The drummers made a huge noise, and the announcer would ask someone to go inside to see if Loong were stirring from his year-long sleep.

We waited. They emerged.

'No. He's still asleep.'

The noise and dancing intensified; Loong was peeped at again, and eventually, the message came back, 'Yes!' He's waking and moving around a little in there.'

We learnt over the years that Loong always took a full day to wake up and get ready for the procession the next day. I liked to think of his coloured coils stirring sleepily in that little house and walked back to the car happily with my eyes and ears full of noise and excitement.

Loong snaked along at the end of the Monday procession, goaded by the two sea lions. His head danced and waved in response to them, and I loved seeing the dance of the three dragon heads. His long silky body undulated behind, seemingly as long as a block of shops and held aloft by a long row of men hidden in his belly. We only saw their black-trousered legs. His glittering tail was long and rigid and needed at least a couple of men to carry it. They always looked very hot.

I thought he was wonderful, but the grown-ups would say to each other, 'Loong is looking a bit tired these days.' They meant that his silky body was faded and a bit tatty and that his sewn on mirrors weren't bright. Poor Loong. He probably did need to go back to his dark little house to sleep for another year.

Loong retired in 1970 and now rests in public view at the Golden Dragon Museum in Melbourne. His successor, Sun Loong, is bright and huge, a hundred metres long and the longest imperial dragon in the world.

When I look back as an adult, I realise that I didn't know any Chinese children, nor did I see anything Chinese throughout the year. It's strange to think that I only knew of their presence in the town because of the dragons at Easter.

When we were a bit older, Mum and Dad sometimes took us into the Saturday evening street carnival. It was dark and the main block of streets was filled with noisy brightly lit stalls and some rides. You knew you wouldn't win anything on the games like the clowns with moving heads or the spinning wheel. I would have liked to have a go on the shooting gallery but wasn't allowed. I had outgrown the merry go round by then and loved the ride where we were whizzed around high above the street in metal seats dangling from long chains.

One year, when Mum and Dad wanted to go home with the smaller children, I still had some spending money left. I said I would be just a quarter of an hour, and they agreed to go back and wait in the car where we'd parked outside the conservatory. I spent and lost money on the clowns and had just enough for the spinning wheel so bought my ticket and watched the giant wheel riffling past the numbers. My number, eighty-four, was up near the top. The wheel started to slow; the loudspeaker commentary got louder; the wheel passed my number once and then slowed and slowed on the next circuit until it nudged right up to eighty-four and stopped!

I'd won! I never won anything. But I had! I had thought about my prizes before I bought the ticket and, when they asked what I wanted, quickly pointed out a multi-coloured leather pouffe and a small BBQ in a box. I thought that the family and I would like those things. They were a bit of a load to carry, but I headed off down Mitchell Street towards the car feeling very proud of myself.

That was short-lived. My stomach suddenly felt really strange and started to sort of jump. 'Oh, no! I'm going to be sick.' I just had time to put my prizes down before all my Easter eggs and dinner heaved up into the gutter at the back of a stall. I stood back, feeling better but a bit conspicuous standing in front of a pile of vomit and a stack of side show prizes.

'Are you alright, love?' asked a lady on the footpath.

'Yes, thanks. I think I had too many Easter eggs'.

I loaded up again with my trophies and got back to the car as fast as I could. There they were, all piled in and waiting. Dad opened the window as I approached.

'Look what I won! AND I was sick in the gutter.'

After the procession on Mondays, I liked to follow the crowd up to the show grounds, where all the street stalls had moved to after Saturday night. Mum and Dad didn't like to do that much, so I had to wait till I was about ten before they'd let me go by myself. It was fun to see all the rides and stalls spread out up there, and sometimes there would be some that hadn't been down on the street on Saturday.

I was careful with the pocket money that I'd saved up. Once

on the ghost train was enough – it was fake scary but I was glad to have tried it. Once only was also good enough for the flea circus. Even with the big magnifying glass, it was hard to know what the fleas were actually doing amongst the tiny toys. I never went into the 'bearded lady' or the 'half-man half-woman' stalls.

I loved the feeling of the Gravitron where the whizzing stuck us to the walls like squashed insects. It was astonishing to be unable even to slide my arm sideways, and the slipping down when the machine slowed was very strange. The whizzy chairs on chains were always good for a repeat, and it felt different to be flying above all the spread-out tents compared to being in the street on the Saturday.

There was always drumming from the front of the large boxing tent. It had a high platform for the drummer and the announcer and the boxers to parade on. There'd be a lot of talking and revving up of the crowd before the boxers were introduced. They'd come from behind a curtain wearing bright satin dressing gowns over their big satin shorts. They wore coloured soft boots and punched the air with their big round boxing gloves. Men and boys went into this tent. I never did.

When I got tired of the sideshows and rides, I'd buy some fairy floss and sit on the benches around the oval and running track to watch the athletics. It was good to have a rest before heading off to the tram stop and home.

The annual emergence of the dragon and the transient flashy rides and stalls of the Easter fair came and went. Their efflorescence provided an exotic and slightly wild element to our normally staid lives.

The foreign country that we knew most about was England. I knew that there were two princesses in England because Mum would talk about them. My first name, Elizabeth, was the name of the older princess and my second name, Margaret, was the same as her younger sister. I had two princess names! I felt a bit silly when I realised that.

I liked Elizabeth because it could shorten to Liz, but not Margaret. It was a boring name. Both names were too long to write, especially when I put my surname, Trembath, on the end. Sometimes, there wouldn't be enough room on the line to fit all those letters and syllables.

Mum told me that when she was in hospital after having had me and named me Elizabeth Margaret, a nurse said to her, 'You must love the royal family!' Mum was really surprised by what she'd done. Her middle name was Margaret and, having lost her surname by getting married, all she wanted to do was to have a part of her carried on to the next generation.

When I was eight, there was a lot of talk about this older Princess being crowned and having a coronation, which would be like a huge church service in a church called Westminster Abbey in London. Mum told us that someone called Norman Hartnell was designing a special long dress for her to wear while she was being crowned, and it had to be decorated with embroidered pictures of the flowers of all the different parts of the United Kingdom. To represent Scotland, there was a thistle, which was quite easy to make look pretty. England's rose was no problem, nor the four-leaved clover, called a shamrock, for Ireland. But the big problem was Wales, which had a leek to represent it – a leek! It also had a daffodil, but Hartnell wasn't allowed to use that. We talked and laughed about how hard it would be to make a muddy leek look good enough for special dress. However, Hartnell managed and Mum was relieved. We saw the dress in magazines, and the leek did look very pretty, though curlier than usual, the way he designed it.

Mum also told us that the crown that would be put on her head was very heavy. We saw pictures of it and were amazed at how huge the jewels were. I had no idea that jewels could be that big. I loved Mum's emerald engagement ring, but the stone in it was tiny compared to those big sapphires and rubies in the crown. You wouldn't have even been able to see her emerald amongst them.

The coronation happened without me really noticing, but one day after school, Mum gathered us on to the couch in the drawing room to show us a special book she had bought. The postie had delivered it. It was full of coloured pictures of Princess Elizabeth who was now Queen Elizabeth and scenes of the service in Westminster Abbey. I looked for the leeks on the dress and found them on a small section on the Queen's tummy. Mum didn't often buy books for herself, and she was very pleased with it.

We kept on hearing about the new Queen and Prince Phillip in the news, and then we learnt that there would be a royal visit next year, 1954. People seemed very excited about that, and I got a bit more interested when we learnt that she would be coming to Bendigo. Mum bought a string of alternating Union Jack and Australian flags to string along the front verandah of our house. At school, we were told that on the special day, we would all be going to the oval at the top of View Street, where they played footie and cricket. The Queen would come there after she had visited lots of other towns so that we could look at her and wave and cheer. I liked the idea of seeing the real person behind all those photos.

One sunny afternoon, we walked in a school crocodile up to the oval and were led to our section on the grass. The entire oval was packed with children by the time all the schools had squeezed into their sections. Mum, Dad and Richard were sitting up in the grandstand somewhere. The way the school kids were placed made a sort of green road where the Queen would drive. But first she had to arrive at Bendigo Station in her special train. We waited. And we waited. It got to after going-home-from school time! Just when I thought I couldn't stand any more waiting, we heard cheering and shouting from down near the Fountain.

'They're coming!'

Suddenly, we were full of energy again. We peered towards the entrance gates and jumped up and down trying to see something. Then the shouting became really loud; the cars had arrived at the gates. Kids were yelling and saying. 'Where are they?' We couldn't see a thing but sort of knew that the cars were driving up and down the green grass roads getting closer to us.

'There they are!' Some ordinary cars came past from our right and then a jeep with a small lady and a tall man standing in the back and waving calmly at us. We weren't calm. We jumped up and down and yelled, 'Hooray'. In seconds, they had gone!

There was a big announcement saying that the footie ground was now the Queen Elizabeth Oval. I liked the idea of that.

The tram home that afternoon was very crowded and happy. Everyone had a story to tell.

I was sure that Prince Phillip had smiled at me personally, but next day at school, every girl was sure that the Queen or Prince Phillip had smiled specially at them. 'How did they do that?' I wondered.

I was starting to realise that although Eaglehawk and Bendigo were big in my world, they were a very small part of the real world that I saw on the globe at school and in the big flat maps on the back wall of the classroom. I'd look at these maps and see huge areas coloured pink which meant that England – it was easier to say 'England' than 'Great Britain' – owned or ruled all those countries. In a way, I was proud to be part of all that pink, but we were so far away from England, all the way down and round the corner on the globe. From my reading, I knew that Australia was very different from small, green England, and I felt that most of us were different from the English. We certainly spoke differently and didn't seem to be so polite or have so many old buildings and history around.

At home, the brown radio sat on a tallish table of its own in the corner between the kitchen and the dining room, the two rooms we used the most. We listened to the ABC's 3LO for music and 3AR for news and the children's programmes. I'd lie on the floor plaiting up the tassels of the rug in a sort of daydream while listening to the *Children's Hour* and *The Muddle-Headed Wombat* stories. We liked the wombat's funny voice. Bendigo's station was 3BO, but we didn't listen to that much.

The radio announcers and news readers had very English-sounding voices and accents and would tell us about things happening in Australia and the world. I started hearing the word Suez a lot but didn't understand why there was fighting. I looked for it on the map and found the canal. I could see that digging a canal would save a lot of time sailing around Africa if you were coming to or from Australia, but still the fighting was too hard for me to understand, and it was a long way away.

The really big news item was that the Melbourne Olympic Games were due to start in November 1956. I was nearly eleven and devoured every news item about them I could find. We had *The Melbourne Age* and The *Bendigo Advertiser* delivered, and

Mum bought *The Australian Women's Weekly* and *Woman's Day* magazines. We learnt about the Olympic torch relay being run all round Australia before ending up in Melbourne, where it would light the big Olympic flame at the new sports stadium.

The torch was going to pass through Bendigo, and the kids from our street thought we'd do our own relay around our own streets. We made a torch with a candle inside a can nailed onto the end of a bit of dowel. The candle didn't stay alight once the bearer started running, but we thought it looked quite good anyway. We'd run up and down outside our place, handing over the torch to the next person. The receiver would practice starting to run slowly with his arm out ready for the current torchbearer to put the torch into it.

The culmination of this was a long run around the entire block with about six changes along the way. We did it one night after dinner. The start was outside our place, and runners jogged off to wait in their positions about a hundred yards apart. Once we got going, it all seemed a bit straggly and not as exciting as it was going to be in our imaginations. I felt a bit lonely and a little bit silly waiting in the dusk and then running along the street by myself carrying a bit of dowel and a tin can.

The newspapers showed us pictures of the Olympic swimming pool being built. I wasn't used to seeing an indoor pool, and this looked very modern with leaning-out walls and a lot of glass. The swimming was going to be exciting as Australia had really good swimmers. We had Dawn Fraser, who always beat Lorraine Crapp, and then there was Faith Leech, who came from Bendigo and used to swim with the Bendigo Swimming Club before she got too good and had to go away to be coached. We hoped that they would come first, second and third in the women's 100 metres event. The men swimmers were good too, but I was following the women.

They won: gold, silver and bronze. I was so proud of Australia and so proud of Faith Leech from Bendigo coming third. Her father owned a jewellery shop in Hargreaves Street, and I would walk past, looking inside, hoping to see my hero. One day, there she was, behind the counter. Her body was so different from any woman's body I knew. She was tall and thin with the widest shoulders I had ever seen. I was awestruck. It was a bit like the Ron Masters moment when I realised I was looking at someone very special.

Television appeared in the year of the Olympics, but we didn't get one. Next door did though, and we watched from our kitchen window as a tall metal pole with a grid of metal strips on top was attached to the chimney and rose high above their roof. This was their aerial. One night, we were asked in to watch the TV. Mum and us kids squeezed through the fence gap, knocked on the back door and were ushered through to their lounge room into a roar of static. The television set was brown and quite small with a screen full of small, flashing white patches.

'There's a bit of snow,' said their dad, adjusting some knobs. Sometimes, we heard a snatch of voice and saw a glimpse of people through what I thought real falling snow would look like. It was a bit embarrassing because there was nothing to see. They got the reception worked out eventually, and Richie would go in and watch with his friend.

Sputnik appeared in 1957. Again, the radio and the newspapers told us about it. There was a bit of a feeling, amongst the excitement, that people would have liked America to get a satellite into space first, but I didn't mind. I liked the name

Sputnik. It sounded and looked exotic with that 'k' without a 'c' in front of it.

We talked about when it would be good to go out and look for it in the night sky, and at last, the night came. After dinner, we went out onto the front footpath and stood with our neighbours looking up at the stars. We easily found the smudgy Milky Way stretched across the clear, inky sky and the points of the Saucepan. That was all our family could identify, though I knew there were lots of other patterns in the sky, such as the Southern Cross.

We had been told to look for a streak across the sky like a fast moving star. We looked and waited, and then, there it was! A thin white light moved from right to left against the blue–black background, not a long line but enough to see that it wasn't a star. It was visible for only a short time, and we waited out there, hoping to see something more. Eventually, we decided that was it; we had seen Sputnik. We walked back up our drives. We were glad to have been out there on our Eaglehawk street taking part in that bit of Russian and world history.

Chapter Thirteen
Dreading School

No kid escapes school!

I'm told that I started kindergarten at Girton at about three years old, but I do not remember a single thing about it. I'm told that I used to catch the tram into Bendigo with a neighbour, who would get off about three stops before my ride ended. She had to go to her work at the hospital in Barnard Street. Apparently, I would stay on the tram and then get off at the Fountain and be met by someone who then took me on to kinder with her child, on the Golden Square tram. Mum has since said that it was a bit much to ask of me. Actually, I don't imagine that I was asked. This was just something that happened to a three-year-old in a tiny brown school uniform. At least, I didn't have to catch the tram home as Mum or Dad would collect me. I imagine that this sometimes involved waiting.

Kindergarten was held in the big old hall. The next year, when I was just four, I started in Infants at the junior school just next to this hall. Junior school was a relatively new cream brick building which consisted of two classrooms and an enclosed verandah at the back, leading outside to the big, rough-grassed open yard, and inside to the cloakroom. The cloakroom was a square windowless and concrete-floored room with three walls furnished with coat hooks, the fourth wall housing three toilets, one of which was very small. There were two low washbasins. The front playground, on a corner, was enclosed by two high street walls, the classrooms and the hall. There were two swings and a see-saw. We could look out on to the street through a wrought iron and cyclone wire driveway gate. A verandah outside the 'big' room covered the steps up to the junior school entrance to the hall.

I'm astonished at how little classroom learning I remember of my first four years of school in the 'little' room. I remember that at the start I was sitting to the left of the room as I faced the teacher. The grades moved up across the room to grade three over by the high windows looking onto the playground. If you were sitting down, these windows allowed you to see only the sky. There might have been about thirty girls in the room, all presided over by the one teacher.

Somehow, I learnt to read and have a very faint memory of sitting in the classroom holding a picture book with a dog and a girl and a boy in it.

However, I do have a very clear memory of plasticine play when I was still over on the very young side of the classroom. We had been given some plasticine to play with and just left to it. The plasticine was old and mushed up and had turned into universal brown. I enjoyed rolling it out into snakes and then tried to see if I could make them stand up to make a little house. Soon, I had four posts and some cross-beams, creating the framework of a tall, narrow room. It was a dunny! I said the word.

'I'm making a dunny.'

The girls sniggered. They all lived in Bendigo and had sewered toilets.

I coiled up some thin snakes to make a little pan to put in the little house. Then I made a little person.

'Look, I'm making a little man, and now he's going to go to the dunny. Trit trot, trit trot.' I jiggled the little figure to the door. More scandalised sniggering, which I enjoyed.

'Now, he's going to sit on the dunny …'

'Elizabeth Trembath! You disgusting girl! You're going to wash your mouth out with soap and water. Come with me!'

The teacher grabbed my hand and pulled me out of the classroom towards the cloakroom.

Soap and water. In my mouth. How peculiar. That'll be horrible, I thought as I was tugged along into the cloakroom. There, I was made to sit on the bench under my coat hook amongst the row of hanging school bags. She turned the light out and shut the door.

'Wait there.'

I did, sitting there in the dark feeling more and more anxious about what was going to happen.

I heard the children being sent out to play in the front yard. I heard her footsteps coming towards me. She pushed open the door and switched on the dim overhead light.

'Now,' she said, 'come here.'

She stood at the basin and handed me a bar of soap. 'Wash your dirty mouth out with that!'

I took the soap. *How do I do this? Do I put it in my mouth?*

She pushed me over the basin and turned on the tap.

'NO!' I shouted and threw the soap away. We faced each other. She tried to grab me again, but I ran to the back of the cloakroom and then round and round shouting amongst the bags and coats with her trying to grab me. Finally, I burst out the door and down into the big yard to hide right in the back corner behind the bushes. No one came after me.

I don't remember how the rest of the day went. I probably went back into class at the end of recess. I don't remember if I told Mum.

I was left feeling guilty for fighting the teacher but eventually proud of myself for fighting back. The punishment was stupid, violent and unfair. I hated things that weren't fair.

As the years crawled by, I have a generalised feeling of my desk moving across the room, and sitting doing goodness knows what for all those hours of the day between playtime and lunchtime and going home time. I must have learnt my tables, learnt how to write letters and then start writing sentences. We must have done drawing and painting.

We used pencils to work with, and usually the teacher sharpened them for us in a little machine with a handle which clamped onto her desk. I went up one day with my blunt pencil to find a queue of younger girls lined up for pencil sharpening.

'Elizabeth, you can do it yourself. Here's the razor.'

I didn't want to do that. I'd never used the special razor with one metal-covered edge and the really sharp blade on the other side.

'I can't do that.'

'Yes, you can. Here it is.'

I took the blade and tried to remember how grown-ups held the pencil in one hand and cut at the wood with the other. I knew to cut facing away from me. My first cut went too deep and made a sharply sloping scoop revealing a facet of pencil wood with quite a length of lead showing. I turned the pencil around a bit and pushed the blade again but not so hard this time. I got a nice smooth angle and then did a couple more.

'There. You did it.'

But I didn't like the result, and felt self-conscious about not doing it all properly and having all that lead showing. Until that pencil went blunt, I made sure that I hid the scoopy side underneath.

One Monday, I took some beautiful bulrush stalks to school to show. I was very excited to have found them growing at the edge of a little dam in the swampy bit below the lake. They had stood straight in the water, looking perfect with their fresh green stalks and leaves and their firm, smooth, velvety brown brushes ending in a little spike.

The teacher was quite pleased and put them in a vase in front of the sunny front windows. During the morning, I liked looking at them and remembering how I found them and was happy to have provided them for the classroom.

After lunch and just before we were to line up to go back in to class for the afternoon, there was a sort of disturbance from the girls already lining up. We ran over and peered in the door.

'Trem's bulrush has exploded!'

There was fluff everywhere. It was magnificent! The floor was fluffy; the desks were covered in parachuted seeds and even the teacher's table was covered in downy mounds. It took ages for us to clean it all up, and I was told not to bring any more bulrushes. I was quietly pleased to have innocently caused such mayhem.

It's curious that I have just three classroom memories from those four years: the plasticine dunny and mouth washing, the pencil sharpening and the bulrush explosion.

However, school did teach me to read. I remember sitting up one night in my bed with my book and looking across at Mum sitting on my younger sister's bed reading to her and my little brother. They were all piled up together with the bed lamp shining over them. I felt a bit envious, because she used to read to me by myself. On the other hand, by then I knew the stories she was reading.

My favourite book had been *Tootle,* a Little Golden Book. I loved the little train with his bright engine and carriages and liked the idea that he had to learn to behave like a train and not jump off his rails and play in the flowery meadows in the sun. I loved his decision to do just that. I was upset at the picture of the field full of men hiding with red flags to make him Stop and Stop and Stop. It was so unfair. I felt sorry for Tootle when he just became like any other grown-up train.

I knew and loved another Golden Book, *Scuffy the Tugboat*, whose adventures ended up in much the same way. He wanted 'bigger things' than the shop and the bathtub, and being a talking tugboat, persuaded his shop owner in the polka dot tie to let him sail in the brook. The brook was running fast, and he was swept away downstream until the sea opened wide in front of him.

'Oh, Oh!' cried Scuffy when he saw the sea. 'There is no beginning and there is no end to the sea. I wish I could find the man with the polka dot tie and his little boy.'

Of course, the man appeared just then, stretching out from a jetty, and picked him up. The last picture was of him happily floating back in the bathtub. I remember asking, 'How did the man know he was there?' and felt it was a bit of a comedown for him to be back in the bathtub.

As an adult, I realise that the sub-text of these books is really about promoting conformity and the curtailment of freedom. That was what had made me feel sad.

The *Wind in the Willows* showed me a world of running rivers and boats. I imagined lots of clean, clear water running in a river which had soft green grass on its banks. I enjoyed meeting a mole and a water rat and a badger who had a very cosy house in the woods and liked the friendship of Ratty and Mole. I would have loved to be in a boat with them tied up to a tree on the river bank, having a magnificent picnic. I was disturbed by Toad's erratic behaviour.

The *Dr Dolittle* books by Hugh Lofting were also about

animals and were interesting and intriguing. I liked the fact that he was always on the side of the animals and the way he had a household of friendly, helpful and kind animals. It was fun to read about animals and imagine what it would be like to be something else other than a human.

Nana and Da gave me *Alice's Adventures in Wonderland* and *Alice Through the Looking Glass* for my seventh birthday. I was able to read that myself and was amazed at how brave Alice was in very strange circumstances. I liked the way she grew and shrank and the way the Cheshire Cat's smile lingered in the air. I was a bit frightened by the unpredictability of the Red Queen and the way she shouted all the time.

A bit later, my reading had moved on to Enid Blyton and I couldn't read enough of the worlds she created. The Magic Faraway Tree in *The Enchanted Wood* really excited me because of the climb up to the ladder reaching up into the swirling cloud at the top of the tree. The children and I never knew what land would be waiting at the top. Rereading the book as an adult, I am nervous about getting back to the ladder and the tree before the land moved on. Once, they had to escape off the cloud in a little aeroplane, piloted by the boy, of course.

The Famous Five were wonderful because books kept coming out and the adventures kept happening. I liked the characters, especially George, whose desire to be a boy I easily identified with. Ann was pretty soppy. The other boys were alright but a bit bossy. I'd have liked to have a dog like Timmy. There was a strangely almost absent mother – in fact, in one book she was away for the whole time – which didn't seem to bother anyone much. I only picked this up on an adult reread. These days we'd have a sub-text on 'dealing with a parent in hospital'. Then, it seemed to be a case of 'let's pretend it's not happening'. Father was amiable but fairly disengaged from his children. These children would go out into the countryside, have adventures by themselves and come home safely. I absorbed the idea of 'safe adventures' from those books. They would talk about their plans and consider what they would do to be safe. There was always a lot of discussion.

I could never have enough of *The Famous Five* and would prowl around Every's Newsagent and Bookshop hoping to find a new title. If I was lucky, someone's birthday party would be coming up, and I could buy the book as a gift. I would read it very carefully, not eating, not bending the covers back too far, and only when I'd finished it, would I wrap it.

I got away with it for a while, until at one party, on handing over the now wrapped present, I enthusiastically told the crowd what a good book it was.

'How do you know?' asked a friend.

Oh, no. I'm stuck now.

'I've read it.'

'This one?' asked another friend.

'Yes.'

'When?' she interrogated. 'Have you got one?'

'I read it yesterday.'

'Trem read this before she gave it to Jill,' my bush lawyer friend shouted.

It was pretty embarrassing. However, I kept on with the secret reading of my gift books and was extra careful not to say anything about them as I handed them over. I might even have told a small fib if necessary.

The Famous Five adventures and the landscape amazed me. There were green fields to run over, running streams, cliffs and caves, racing tides that could cut you off – but convenient boats on hand. George even owned an island! And their food was astonishing. There was so much of it, and it was quite different from ours. My brother and sister and I would fall about laughing over 'lashings of custard' and 'lashings of ginger beer'. My children did the same. I'm laughing as I write the words 'lashings of custard'.

The scale of the landscape was different from Australia in that places were closer together and everything was more coherent or connected than our sprawling, untidy, dry, thinly vegetated neighbourhood and countryside.

When I did get to England in my twenties, the rounded heaviness and the greenness of the trees was more dramatic than I had imagined. Streams did run fast and fill the whole stream bed. Grass was soft and green. Roses did drape themselves over thatched cottages, and daffodils did appear in swathes. Best of all, on a Devon beach that seemed to be all sand, I experienced a tide coming in so fast that we had to move our towels almost as soon as we'd noticed the approaching water. Within about thirty minutes, all the beachgoers were piled up together on the bit of dry sand at the top of the bay. Now I understood the anxieties about being 'cut off by the tide'. Our tides never did that so quickly, nor were our beaches so gently shelving.

Reading taught me about adventures and risk taking. My imagination developed as I was taken away from my home in a small inland Australian country town to other homes, places and countries. Without it being an obvious lesson, I was starting to develop empathy and learn about the complexity of life and how people solved problems. I gathered valuable insights into fairness and unfairness

When I was nine, I moved into grade four and the 'big room'. We must have been allowed to choose our own desk within our grade section, and I grabbed the one in the front row right in front of the door with the windows on my left. I knew that sometimes the door would be left open for fresh air, so I'd be able to feel the air and look outside. That was compensation for being at the front, but I was well to Miss Cure's right. I was a bit deaf again (I often seemed to have a cold and had suffered a burst eardrum as a two-year-old) so I wanted to be able to hear. It was embarrassing to miss what the teacher was saying, and I wanted to please this new teacher, as well as me.

Each morning, we would start the day by chanting our tables. I liked that. It settled me down after the rush and lateness to school and was a good, mindless start to the day.

Like all composite classrooms, the blackboard would be set up in sections for the different grades. Miss Cure would introduce or teach each group and leave us to do the sums, or write the story or copy the list while she moved on to the next group. It must have been hard for her but at least we were well behaved.

Once, she set the whole room a memorising task. We were to learn the Twenty-third Psalm by heart. This was boring, I thought. I wanted to be doing a lesson or something proper. Miss Cure settled at her desk, with a pile of exercise books in front of her. She picked up her red marking pencil. I looked at the closed door in front of me. Alright, I'll learn it, FAST, and that will show her. I had a head start because of all my church and Sunday School. A few minutes later I had it. Right, run it through again in my head. Yes, I've got it.

My hand shot up.

'Miss Cure, I've learnt it!'

'Oh, Trem,' the class muttered. I was surprised. They must have liked just sitting there.

'Elizabeth, you couldn't have,' said Miss Cure.

'I have.'

'Oh well, come out the front and show us,' she said, still holding her pencil.

I stood in front of the class, looked at the back wall and rattled off, 'The Lord is my Shepherd ...' to the end. I stopped and turned towards her.

Miss Cure sighed and told me to find something to read.

That was alright because I always had a book in my desk just in case.

We learnt a lot: heaps of arithmetic, lists of spelling and vocabulary, grammar in columns on the blackboard, the countries of the world, poems to recite and sometimes even drawing.

We had been told to prepare for a drawing test. We could think about what we'd like to draw and practice it in preparation for the test. I decided that I would copy an illustration from *Tootle*. I still loved the picture of Tootle the train dancing and playing in the field, off the rails, and feeling free and happy. The Golden Book illustration was a highly coloured double spread, and I looked at it hard and thoroughly in preparation and sharpened my pencils. In the test, which we were allowed to do out in the playground, I loved drawing that picture and was really pleased with how good it looked when I had finished. Tootle was the right size and in the right place and looked happy and bright amongst the grass and bushes and little animals.

The girls really liked it.

Miss Cure looked at my drawing.

'What is this?'

'It's Tootle,' I answered. 'It's a book,' I explained when she looked blank.

'Did you copy it?'

'Nooo! I learnt it.'

'Hmm.'

What did all of that mean? I had done something that wasn't quite right, but I knew that my drawing was good. It was actually hard to get it right with Miss Cure, but I still wanted her to notice me and be nice to me.

When I was about ten, Mum and I decided that it was time to have my plaits cut off. They were about a foot long when plaited up, and I was tired of waiting and standing there in the bathroom each morning getting my hair done. Also, we still hadn't sorted out how to deal with them in swimming races.

After school one day, Mum took me to have my hair cut at the hairdresser's for the first time in my life. I had waited while Jane and Rich had had their hair cut but never sat in the chair in front of the mirror. Mum was a bit excited and nervous and had brought a brown paper bag to take the plaits home in. I sat with a towel around my shoulders; the hairdresser put in a rubber band at the top of each plait and, with some very sharp scissors, just cut the first one off with a sort of crunchy sound, handed it to Mum and did the same with the other. It was strange seeing the two dismembered plaits lying there. They suddenly weren't part of me.

By the way, Mum kept the plaits in the same brown paper bag and, during some tidying up about forty years later, handed them over to me. I still have them. The hair looks fresh and bright, and I haven't a clue about what to do with them!

In the mirror, my hair was a funny shape, but the hairdresser cut it so that I had a head of short curly hair. It felt light and free and I liked it.

Next morning, I brushed it by myself and went off to school to show it to all my friends.

'Ooh, Trem's had a haircut.'

There was a bit of talk about it and then it was time for prayers. Afterwards, when it was time to line up to go into class, Miss

Cure still hadn't said anything my new appearance, so I jiggled around in front of her and said, 'Miss Cure, I've had a haircut.'

She looked down at me and paused.

'Very nice, Elizabeth,' she finally replied, in her thin, high, tight voice. And that was that! I felt a bit disappointed.

At home, Mum's new baby had finally arrived. She had been getting bigger and bigger, and her tummy felt tight and hard when I hugged her. She was getting really tired after dinner and the washing up and sat on the couch with her feet up. Dad woke us early one morning to say that he was taking Mum to the hospital to have the baby. It was a wintry morning, just light, and the three of us gathered at our bedroom window and waved and called out, 'Good bye, Mummy,' to the car as it backed down the drive. Mum looked bundled up and uncomfortable and didn't wave back. Soon there was a knock on the door, and Mary, from over the road, who sometimes helped with the housework, came in to get us ready for school. She did this so efficiently that I was on the early tram and at school before I knew what had happened. When we got home that afternoon, Dad told us that we had a new sister called Sally.

That night, after dinner, he took us all in to the hospital. We all wanted to see our new little sister, but we had to stand in a corridor and look at a room full of babies wrapped up and lying in metal bassinets. We could hear a lot of babies crying. A nurse saw us, went to a bassinet and picked up a tightly wrapped bundle, which she brought over to the window. We couldn't see much so she angled herself to show our little sister's face. We looked and didn't really know what to say or think. Her eyes were closed; she looked a bit pink and very small. We said, 'Hello Sally,' waved at her, and she was taken back to her bed.

Our family was now complete. Six was a good number, and I liked the idea of us being four children.

Next morning, Mary came over again to help us off to school, and again I was early and happy. One of my classmates came up and said, 'Congratulations, Trem.'

Oh, I thought, what for? Is she sarcastic about me being early?

'Thanks, I was really early again this morning.'

'No, Trem!' She was pretty fed up with me. 'Congratulations on your new baby!'

'Oh. Thank you.'

How was I to know? I hadn't had the baby, Mum did. How did they know to say such a grown-up thing? I felt really stupid.

When we were lining up for class, Miss Cure looked at me and also congratulated me. This time, I knew what it was about and said thank you nicely.

I always raced through the work to get it finished as fast as I could. That was annoying for Miss Cure because of the problem of what to do with me then. My writing wasn't neat because I couldn't make all the letters slope evenly, and my very best efforts didn't please even me much. If I'd been able to make my writing look good, I'd have done just that, but couldn't, so I was happy enough. Miss Cure wasn't.

I had finished a composition and stood at her desk for her to check it.

'Elizabeth, what do you call this! Look at the mess!'

Well, it was a bit blotchy and scrabbly.

'But it's finished. And look, I've got sentences and proper paragraphs.' I knew that I had learnt the lesson and that my story, if read aloud, would have shown this. All she could see was the mess.

I used to have to stay in so many times and copy things out again. There'd be a little group of us parked in the back seats, sighing and resentful. At least, I was only copying and not struggling with brain work and getting things right at that end of the day. I'd get pretty angry when sent back to recopy my first after-school effort.

One afternoon as I was copying something out yet again, I was getting annoyed with the nib of my pen, which kept crossing and splattering ink over the work, and suddenly had an idea. I'd been longing for a fountain pen, but we weren't allowed to have one in junior school. I thought that I might be able to persuade Mum to persuade Miss Cure to let me have a fountain pen because it would make my writing better. To my astonishment, both agreed, and one afternoon after school, I went to Every's Newsagent and Bookshop with Mum to buy a fountain pen. The pens sat in rows behind glass, a bit like rings at the jewellers. The salesman brought out a few for me to try. I loved the navy blue Conway Stewart. The blue was mixed with black in a splotchy sort of pattern and made the gold nib and gold trim round the lid and clip look rich and shiny. I was allowed to buy it and went home with it clipped into my blazer pocket. I also bought a bottle of Royal Blue Quink ink, which the salesman said was better for the pen than the Swan ink we had at school.

My writing improved a bit, simply because I took more care with my beautiful pen.

I wished Miss Cure had been able to see past the appearance to the essence of my work and sometimes give me some praise. I wanted to do the work and wanted to learn, but the classroom was dull and awful and seemed to need constant negotiation.

A year later, I chose the back row. Too bad if sometimes I couldn't hear. It felt more private with my back to the wall.

We had a performance, once, where the junior school was doing something Dutch. I arrived at the back door of the school theatre in a dress with a white apron and a sort of white cap with Dutch-type detail around the ears. With my blond hair in plaits, I thought I looked quite fitting. That was until I saw my windmill again.

Part of our item was to walk around holding Dutch windmills as we sang. I thought that was a bit silly but was putting up with it. My grandfather had made my windmill for me. I'd told Da what Miss Cure had said to do. He had questioned me thoroughly and set to work.

I took my white-painted windmill to school for the dress rehearsal. 'What's that?' my friends asked.

'Oh!' said Miss Cure. 'Well, we'll stand it at the back.'

The classroom was bristling with huge multi-coloured two-dimensional windmills. Some had sails that could turn, and most had elaborately painted detail. Mine was white and skeletal. It was a pole, mounted at the top with a small cross of two similar bits of wood to represent the sails. My sails did at least turn.

I didn't know why my understanding of what Miss Cure had asked for differed so hugely from the interpretations of the other girls' fathers. I was sure she had talked about something simple. I was sure she had mentioned white. Anyway, I lurked at the back, feeling pretty stupid with my white windmill. I imagine that my grandfather sitting in the audience felt pretty stupid too.

Back in the classroom, grade fives were about to start some more sewing. I'd already made a little sort of green cloth envelope with different stitches on it in dark red thread and hadn't minded doing that too much.

This time, Miss Cure announced that we were going to make petticoats, half slips in fact. I couldn't think of anything worse. I could see there would be miles of boring stitching involved, and I never wore petticoats and only wore a dress to Sunday School and church on sufferance.

I announced the impending horror to Mum, who would have to buy the material. She chose some fine white fabric with a tiny red spot on it. No lace, under strict instructions from me. So it seemed I was going to sew a slimmish tube of material with no adornment – elastic at the top and a small hem at the bottom. I liked the material, even though I was never going to wear it, and thought Mum and I had worked out quite a good compromise.

Sewing afternoon arrived. I arrived with my small, floppy parcel of fabric and watched in amazement as the other girls unpacked yards and yards of dazzling white Swiss cotton covered in embroidery and eyelets and then yards and yards of lace.

'Ooh! What's that?' the girls said about my material.

'Oh!' said Miss Cure. 'That looks more like skirt material to me. You didn't get much.'

Skirt material! I thought. *Don't be stupid. You can see it's too thin for a skirt.*

'Well, I like it,' I said, to save my pride.

So I resigned myself to afternoons of pinning seams and creeping along them doing a grubby uneven backstitch. The whole thing was limp and forlorn by the time I'd finished, and I never wore it. I probably got a terrible mark but didn't care.

That same year, something exciting came up. We were to make scrapbooks. Oh, not for us but for sick children in hospital. Miss Cure wanted us to cut up pretty greeting cards and pictures from magazines, and she showed us some examples with red roses and other flower arrangements.

But if I were stuck in bed, I thought, I wouldn't want to look at pictures of roses. I know. I've got an idea.

'Miss Cure, can we put in cartoons and jokes?'

'Oh, er, no, just keep it like a picture book.'

Well! How boring! I did my scrapbook but tried really hard

to find non-rose pictures and snuck in some cartoons and jokes anyway. I suppose all the scrapbooks went off to the Bendigo Hospital. I wondered if anyone ever looked at mine

Each year as we went up a grade, we would buy a new Victorian Reader. These were produced by The Education Department of Victoria and filled with an astonishing range of literature: patriotic Australian poems and stories extolling our beautiful country and the bush, snippets from the classics (I never did understand why Ulysses had to be tied to the mast), poems and stories about England, some fairy tales and poems about flowers. I remember being pretty frightened by a story about a mine cave-in and flood and how the men had to wait and wait for a rescuer in a full diving suit to reach them. Even the illustration of the helmeted man approaching was sinister. I knew about mines and how dangerous they could be.

The worst stories in the readers were about snakes. In *Rikki-Tikki-Tavi*, I learnt about mongooses and cobras and Indian houses. The atmosphere was tense but the setting a bit remote from my life.

The really frightening stories were the Australian ones.

Henry Lawson's *The Drover's Wife* gave us the endless suspense of that mother's night alone with her children, protecting them from the snake that had slithered into their bush home. I was frightened by the idea of a snake hiding in the house and could feel the mother's terror and isolation and the oldest boy's fear and sense of responsibility.

The other Lawson story was even worse. Two drovers were sleeping by the campfire in their respective swags when one of them realised that a snake had curled up inside his swag next to his body. He quietly woke his friend and they worked out a plan. All the time they were talking, the man with the snake in his swag had to lie motionless to avoid disturbing it. When they were ready, the free man loaded and aimed his gun at where the snake would be in his friend's swag. On a count, the trapped man had to fling off the covers and leap out of the way, enabling the snake to be shot. This happened according to plan.

I was terrified. Even in the classroom. That night, I had to get Mum to pull back my bedcovers so that I could see there was no snake there. And again, the next night. It took a long time to get over that story, and I still think of it with horror.

It made me very wary of snake danger. I am the one who will spot a snake anywhere, but even before I do, I have already spotted a lot of 'snake' sticks and 'snake' bark. But when I actually do see a snake, I have no doubt that it is real – gleaming and alive.

The school library was in a room in the boarding house. Each wall was covered in books that all seemed to have brown, navy or dark red spines. Amongst all those books was a small section against the back wall which had fiction. I read my way through the Billabong books, but I wasn't very interested in them.

Was it in one of these books that a girl had a tree fall across her back, pinning her to the ground in agony all night until she was found next morning? I think she ended up 'a cripple' and was very brave about it all. I was frightened about this 'cripple' idea and met another in *Little Women*. What was it about girls that got them crippled and why were they so cheerful in their beds and wheelchairs? Boys didn't seem to get crippled while having adventures.

There was an even longer row of books by Charles Dickens to try. They were hard, but I met David Copperfield and was astonished and horrified by his life and his English world. I liked the humour of Mr Micawber and his faith that 'something will turn up'. I knew it wouldn't, and that was suspenseful and painful. Oliver Twist lived an extraordinary life too. Eaglehawk had poor families, but it was nothing like those times and places.

There actually wasn't much to read in that library, but I came to realise that the cream brick building near the Bendigo Town Hall was a library. I went there by myself one day after school, feeling a bit anxious about this new territory. Inside, it was light and cheerful with colourful books everywhere. They were in shelves around the walls and in bookshelves standing in rows in the middle of the floor. So many books! There were even some tables where grown-ups were sitting and looking at books or reading newspapers.

I found some books I wanted to read and saw that there was a desk with a lady who was stamping the books loudly as people came up to borrow them. I stood in a queue and, when it was my turn, handed the books to the librarian. I was a bit nervous by then because I had seen that the people in front of me were handing over a card.

'Where's your library card?'

'I haven't got one.'

'You'll have to get your mother to get you one. Where do you live?'

'Church Street, Eaglehawk.'

'Oh. You can't borrow books from here if you live in Eaglehawk. This is the Bendigo Library.'

'Oh.'

That was embarrassing and disappointing and I didn't understand. It seemed like a long tram trip home before I could tell Mum what had happened. She said that it must be because Eaglehawk was separate from Bendigo and had its own council.

I think we might have had a library, but it seemed as though it wasn't a possibility for me. However, Mum did get me a library card. She rang the library and found that if a resident of Bendigo were prepared to sponsor or guarantee me, the Bendigo Library would issue me with a card. So she rang a Bendigo friend who agreed to do that, and then she must have sorted out all the forms. I was so happy to get that card and loved going to the library. Mum and I did well to manage all that.

Back to the classroom! We were far too afraid of Miss Cure to misbehave or do anything much out of line. One day, I'd forgotten to go to the toilet at lunchtime, and not long into the afternoon, I really needed to go. Miss Cure would get cross if you put your hand up to go to the toilet, but I just had to. I was still in grade give and she was teaching the grade sixes. I put my hand up. She ignored me. I kept it up. I waved it around a bit. I tried to catch her eye. I waited and waited and it got worse and worse. She did not allow you to interrupt her, and I was too scared to get out of my place and just run out the door. Finally, I had to let go. I felt the wet warmth run down my legs on to the wooden chair seat and flow on to the dry wooden floor in an ever enlarging dark puddle.

'Oh Trem,' said the girls next to me, screwing up their faces and moving away. Miss Cure finally noticed my bright red mortified face. It must have got sorted out somehow.

I sat in that classroom for another year, hating it and the teacher. I longed to be sick so that I could stay at home, but that hardly ever happened. I would be sent off to school with stupendous colds and my blazer pockets full of torn-up squares of old sheets because we'd run out of clean hankies.

Writing this, my heart became heavier and heavier as I thought about myself, over sixty years ago, eager to learn, full of ideas and wanting approval. I wondered how on earth that child managed to keep going and be fairly cheerful most of the time.

Then I realised that the best things at school happened outside the classroom and that playtime was enough to keep me afloat during the times inside.

Chapter Fourteen
Out Of The Classroom

We did have some lessons outside the classroom and met teachers who weren't Miss Cure!

Once a week, we would change into our sports uniform, a short pale blue tunic worn over a short-sleeved white blouse, and go into the hall. I was in Ahern House and therefore had a gold sash to tie around my waist. I liked learning how to tie the knot correctly and have it just to the left of centre. The sash was a sort of silky rope with soft, shiny tassels at each end. I would arrange the tying so that one tassel hung slightly lower than the other.

We would line up with our backs to the side wall with the tallest girl near the stage, moving down to the shortest. Mr Meredith, the visiting teacher, would tell us to reach out our left arm to the shoulder of the girl beside us and shuffle down until our arm was straight. Then we would take one step to the left and turn to the front. We had to wait for his order at each stage. When we were quiet, he would turn on his big tape recorder and marching music would start.

'Ready, girls. Quick march! Left, right, left, right!'

And off we'd go, trying to keep in step and remembering to swing our arms. I loved it. It was a bit like chanting the tables but better because I was up and doing something with my body. After a few circuits of the hall, we'd start peeling off in rows of six, facing the front and making a nice pattern of rows. We'd keep marching on the spot till the last girls got into place, and then Mr Meredith would call, 'Claaass. Halt!' Sometimes, we got the 'Halt' done all together.

Then it was time to 'do our exercises'. I think they'd be called calisthenics, but I never heard that word mentioned. I liked doing these too. I'd copy Mr Meredith to get the movements right and liked repeating them in time to the music. His music was always cheerful. I'd lift my arms high on 'One' and on 'Two' bring them down parallel to my shoulders. 'Three' would be swinging my right hand to my left foot and so on. I enjoyed getting the movements crisp and accurate and being moved towards the front because I was doing well.

Mr Meredith was energetic and encouraging. He was always dressed in white, and in summer he changed from his long white pants to white shorts. His legs were brown and muscly, and we'd all get a bit excited about their first summer showing.

These calisthenics would be part of the occasional concert the school put on in the hall. It was a good change from classroom routine to have rehearsals and then be out at night in the dark with all the lights on the stage and the hall full of parents murmuring away on the other side of the dark blue curtain. We would peep out from the side of the curtain to try and find where our families were sitting.

One year, the song 'I Love to Go a-Wandering' was on the radio a lot. I learnt the words and enjoyed singing the *Val-de-ri, Val-de-ra* chorus along with the radio. When this year's concert was announced, we were told that this time we were allowed to offer items. Some girls decided to play the piano; one would recite an elocution poem; some would sing rather soppy songs, and I thought I would sing *The Happy Wanderer*.

We didn't have a full rehearsal (how risky was that!), just a walk-through of the order of items, so when I arrived backstage in my shorts, check shirt, little backpack and stick, Miss Cure was rather surprised by my costume.

'But you're in shorts!'

'Yes, it's a song about walking.'

'Hmm.'

My turn came. I walked on to the stage. The piano started and I burst forth into a very enthusiastic performance.

I love to go a-wandering,
Along the mountain track.
And, as I go, I love to sing,
My knapsack on my back.

I did some self-choreographed marching on the spot during the *Val-de-ri, Val-de-ras* and *Ha-Ha-Has* of the chorus. There was a lot of applause and I was very happy. Knowing what I know now about my lack of tunefulness and remembering that a few years later I was told to just mouth the words in the school choir on concert nights, I realise that people had been very kind to me.

The best thing about grade six, apart from moving closer to the wood-burning stove, was being allowed to start learning tennis up at the senior school. Senior school was actually up the hill and separated from us by a big brick wall and the backs of its buildings. We went up a dirt ramp under the pepper trees, through an opening in the wall and emerged into the senior school with its tennis court on the left, the weatherboard boarding house rising to the right and the classrooms ahead. Mr Sleeman came up from Melbourne every third Friday to give lessons. We'd be allocated a time on the school notice board that morning, so I would run up the ramp before school, find my lesson time and wait in class, checking my watch until it was time to be excused, change into my sports tunic and run up for my lesson.

I brought Mum's old racket, but Mr Sleeman sometimes lent me one that was a bit lighter, until I got my own a couple of years later. He taught well, and I enjoyed being in the little group of girls learning how to serve, do a forehand and backhand, a half-volley and a volley, the scoring and the rules. I was able to practise against the laundry wall at home and enjoyed improving.

He was always patient and respectful to me. Once, I was having trouble hearing what he was saying from half a court away, deaf again, and he came closer and said, 'I'm sorry. Are you having trouble hearing me?' I became pink and teary and embarrassed. He came right up to me and said in a positive, natural way, 'That's alright. I'll just speak a bit louder. You should always tell me.' That felt so good.

Anything that took us out of the classroom was wonderful, and there was a day when Miss Cure announced that we were all going to clean the classroom windows. I was a bit torn. For one thing, it was a morning out of the classroom, but on the other hand, I didn't actually want to clean. However, there was no choice and we all ran outside.

There were a lot of small panes, and for a while, it was fun smearing the white Bon Ami paste over the glass and drawing with our fingers through the white. It was quite fun wiping it off with crumpled up newspaper and seeing the clean window emerge. We were all competing to do the windows we could reach as there was a shortage of chairs to stand on for the higher windows.

Aha! I spotted a row of windows above the verandah roof. This was an excuse to climb up there and do something different – and maybe annoy Miss Cure a bit.

So, I got some Bon Ami and a wet cloth and threw them up onto the roof. It was a new climb from the railings near the hall steps, up the verandah supports and a heave up to the roof. Up there, I could see over the school wall across the street through the straggly elms to Milne's workshop roller door. It was too dark inside to see what they were working on. I could see Miss Cure's weatherboard cottage a few doors up on the street to the side of Milne's. I was now higher than the big timber supports of the playground swings.

The verandah was wide and strong and perfectly safe, so I started work whitening a row of window panes. It was fun to see the desk tops in the deserted classroom from above, and I was enjoying just being up there.

It didn't last for long. The giggling got louder and then …

'Elizabeth Trembath. Come down at once.'

I stood and looked down on the school yard. Miss Cure, in her brown clothes, stood in a sea of girls. There were now many faces looking up.

'I'm cleaning the windows.'

'Not up there. I didn't tell you to clean up there. Come down.'

'But they're dirty!'

'It's dangerous. Come down at once!'

Pause.

'Will I wipe off the Bon Ami or will I come straight away?'

Pause.

'Wipe the Bon Ami off and then get down and come and see me at my desk!'

It was a good morning after all!

The playground swings were terrific. Like the ones down at the Eaglehawk Park, the seat was supported by rigid iron rods which meant that we could go really high. I loved pushing up higher and higher, hearing the creaking and groaning and sometimes being higher than horizontal, or at least that's what it felt like. It was fun also to be a pusher because, once I got the swing going really high, I could grab the seat on its way back past me, and the momentum would lift me into the air as it continued rising. Then, when I'd land, I'd push it off again.

The see-saws were alright, and the best fun on them was to try to bump the other girl off with a little jolt at my grounding moment. I loved it when my partner would do the jolt. I'd let go, fly into the air and then land again on the plank to give it the impetus to go down. You actually didn't do this with someone who didn't like it.

Rounders and dodgie were two games we learnt in sport. These were really good because we could play them at lunchtime. We'd mark out a big dodgie rectangle in the front playground, pick our teams, choose the throwers for each end and toss to see who went 'in' first. Being a thrower was great because you didn't have to stand on the side and wait until the other team all got tagged and out. The rules were simple. You aimed a basketball at the people who were 'in', maybe about a dozen to start with. If the ball hit a girl, she was 'out' and had to stand outside the court. If someone caught a ball on the full, she could call 'in' one of her 'out' team members. The thrower could do a huge, high throw to the other end, and if it were caught on the full by the other thrower, she'd yell 'stop' and everyone on court would freeze. Then we could throw at anyone and get her out. You'd usually aim for one of their agile, good catchers. I loved being on the court and dodging the ball and sometimes catching it. It was a good game because everyone could play, and the rules were so clear and simple.

Like most of our games, it went in crazes. We'd do nothing but play dodgie for weeks, and then suddenly it'd be skipping with a long rope. I liked skipping and enjoyed the various ways we could play: counting the number of skips before you went out, raising the rope higher and higher until you couldn't jump it any more, skipping faster and faster until the rope whipped your legs at last, running through in various ways or jumping with two ropes crossing like an eggbeater. Skipping was good because we could do it at home if someone turned for you. If you only had two people you could tie one end to a tree or pole or, if I were by myself, there was always single rope skipping.

Hoppie, hopscotch, would materialise at some unknown signal, and the yard would be covered in hoppie games. I would carry around two taws in my blazer pocket during the hoppie season. One was a largish blocky bit of mullock, about the size of a big, square Uneeda biscuit but higher, that lay flat and could be kicked smoothly around the boxy grid. For the other game, where throwing accurately into a base was important, I would have a smaller, lighter tor. This was another game that we could play at home.

Rounders happened down in the big yard. I liked it because it was a bat and ball game, and it was fun to use the little bat and tennis ball in contrast to dodgie's basketball.

The big yard had some large old pepper trees around near the ramp up to senior school and the high red-brick wall at the back of the tennis court. Some of the trees drooped to the ground, making little green caves and cubbies. It felt very dramatic to run through the curtains of trailing leaves and either burst in or burst out to the yard with peppery leaves trailing over my shoulders.

The bigger trees up near the wall were hard to climb, but I could actually get up one and then on to the top of the wall. It was probably about five yards high on our side but only a couple of yards high at the back of the tennis court. I could climb along the wall and gradually end up in the far back corner of the yard. The smooth top of the wall had started to break up here and the two rows of dry and crumbly bricks were separate and parallel to each other as the wall stepped down to the corner. Mostly, the teachers didn't know about these climbs, but once, one of the senior school teachers saw me when I was on a branch near the ramp and told me to get down.

One of the best seasonal events in the playground was the making of the Easter nests for the Easter bunny. We would gather huge armfuls of grass from the bottom yard (I wonder if they put off mowing for that reason) and shape them into large round nests to attract the bunny. There must have been an amazing amount of grass because we made a lot of nests. We would choose the location, rip off the grass and lay a circular base, maybe a yard in diameter and build up thick, soft walls to about a foot high. I can't remember if we decorated them with flowers at school, but we certainly did that with our nests at home.

It would be really exciting on the afternoon of the Thursday before Good Friday because we knew that the bunny, the teacher from the other room, would be sneaking out to put eggs in our nests. Then Miss Cure would make the much anticipated surprise announcement that she thought she'd heard the Easter bunny and would we like to go to look? Of course we would, and out we'd race to find beautifully shiny foil-covered eggs tucked carefully in each of the nests. There would be one each. Then we would be allowed to pack up and go home early for the Easter holiday.

The playground kept me going. I would play and play and play at recess and lunchtime and come back to class exhilarated, happy and ready to face whatever happened next.

Chapter Fifteen
Liking School

Senior school was completely different from junior school. For the first time we had a different teacher for each subject, and the subjects had names: English, science, French, mathematics, geography, history and so on. Not only that, there was a timetable which we could write down, and we would know in advance what lesson we would have on what day and at what time. We had many different exercise books and text books. It was all new and exciting.

The classrooms were set in a row inside a long, cream-painted weatherboard building fronted by a deep verandah. The cloakroom at the end of the verandah, near the First Form classroom, was open, light and airy. A few yards in front of the verandah, a solid concrete wall about five feet high terraced up the lawn and garden behind it. We could lie on the grass eating our lunch, surrounded by flowering shrubs and trees, and we could always see some garden from our desks.

The first day back at school after the summer holidays, we were herded into our form groups under the verandah, where we all fitted because the school was very small. I think there were only about a hundred girls in senior school. The junior school marched up, and we had prayers, all spread out wide in front of the headmistress. We were then introduced to our form mistress, Mrs Reilly, who was new to the school.

When it was time to go in to the form room, I raced down to the back corner and grabbed a double desk all for myself, near the windows. This would now be mine. I would be able to see everything yet feel private in my corner. We were going to have this room all to ourselves and not have to share it with the other grades. Mrs Reilly walked in carrying an armful of books and folders. We stopped talking and stood to attention, staring at her.

'Good morning, girls.'

'Good morning, Mrs Reilly,' we bounced back.

'Sit down.'

She had already sounded different, but once she started talking to us, it was lovely. She had a light voice, and the way she spoke and pronounced words sounded pretty and soft. She said that she came from Ireland and was looking forward to getting to know us. She had dark hair and looked comfortably motherly with a bosom and hips. I liked her immediately.

She had a brilliant idea, which was that we could each paint our desk in whatever colour we liked. I wanted a blue one. So Mum took me up to Fitzpatrick's, and we looked at cards of paint colours, all sorts of blues with all sorts of names. I liked Sky Blue.

Mum said, 'It's a bit bright.'

I said, 'That doesn't matter. We're allowed to have what we want.'

So we bought a tin of the Sky Blue and a brush, ready for the painting day.

Some of the single desks were carried out to be painted on to the verandah to allow room inside for us to paint the others. I was given newspaper to put on the floor under mine, which I had moved out from the corner. Then I opened my tin and saw the beautiful bright blue lying in there waiting to be stirred up ready for the paint brush. I knew about painting because I had painted bits of my cubby. I stirred up the paint with a stick, dipped the brush in, wiped it on the rim and laid the first sweep of colour across the desk top. The brown wood succumbed to the blue paint and quite soon my desk sat there, transformed into a cheerful, bright sky blue. I loved it. The other desks emerged as mostly murky dark greens, blues and maroons. I thought they were still a bit dreary, but the furniture was all much more interesting than before.

I had a friend in the front seat of my row, and during class we used to pass secret notes to each other via the girls in between – just because we could! Then I thought that it would be fun to rig up a little pulley system along the wall side of our desks to transport the notes. There were just two girls in between, and they thought that would be fun too. So I brought along some little nails and hammered two, one above the other into the sides of my desk, and the same into the front row desk. I looped some string around the nails and we had a basic system set up. Attaching the notes was a bit trickier but I worked that out and we had a trial run during our next English lesson with Mrs Reilly. I was too scared to try it with any of the other teachers, who weren't as good-humoured.

It worked well and I enjoyed just gently tugging the string to deliver and receive notes while we were doing our work. After a couple of lessons, I was so delighted with it that I couldn't resist showing it to Mrs Reilly after class. She laughed and laughed and said something like, 'Just don't get caught.' Soon after that, the novelty wore off, and we ran out of things to say in our notes. One day, I just dismantled it.

With Mrs Reilly, English was interesting and enjoyable. We read Paul Gallico's *Jennie*, which was a completely new sort of book to me. The way he turned from a boy into a cat was difficult to understand because I didn't know what was real and what was fantasy. The book also talked about the boy/cat's real feelings about his mother and his loneliness. It was hard to answer the questions we were asked, but I liked having to think about something that wasn't easy. She would read aloud other books and stories to us, and I would put my head down on my arms on the desk top and just listen to her lively, pleasant voice and fall into the stories. We did all the basic stuff like spelling, dictation, grammar and vocabulary, but it seemed to fit gently around the edge of the good bits of composition and reading.

All this is not to say that my inner smart alec was at bay. For one of our poetry lessons, she invited us to choose a poem from our textbook and come out to the front to read to the class. I had previously discovered the epic length of 'The Rime of the Ancient Mariner' and decided to try it on. Up went my hand and soon it was my turn.

'What are you going to read, Elizabeth?'

'The Rime of the Ancient Mariner.'

A couple of groans from the class. A funny look from Mrs Reilly. So off I went!

'It is an ancient Mariner,

And he stoppeth one of three.'

And on and on and on. I got past the shooting of the albatross and the 'water, water, every where,' bit and was starting to wonder when I'd be stopped. Finally, I think we were all relieved when Mrs Reilly interrupted, thanked me, and I went back to my desk.

The feeling of that little tease was quite different from the defiance of the 'Twenty-third Psalm' episode with Miss Cure. This felt more like a joke, and it was accepted as such.

A bit later in the year, Mrs Reilly suggested that we might like to have some pen pals with some boys in a boys' home at a place called Phillip Island. She explained that she had two sons who were living there because she was not allowed to have them living with her while she was a house mistress for our boarders. We liked that idea and a couple of lucky girls 'won' her sons in the draw for our pen pals. For a while, we sent off letters to our pen pals and occasionally got letters back. My pen pal didn't seem to have much to say to me, nor me to him.

Then Mrs Reilly announced that we were allowed to go on an overnight excursion to visit the boys at their boys' home. Mum said that I could go, and we eventually set off on the train from Bendigo Station. It was an adventure to be on the train going so far away and to a new place. When we arrived in Melbourne, we had to wait quite a while at the station before we could catch the little train to the stop nearest Phillip Island.

I was getting tired, restless and hungry waiting on the station benches at the end of the afternoon when I noticed that a man had come up to Mrs Reilly and was talking to her. His clothes looked untidy and a bit dirty; he was noisy and restless, and we realised that he was drunk. What would she do? Suddenly we stopped scuffling around, and all eyes were on them. She didn't look pleased and was trying to quieten him down. He was nearly shouting at her, going on and on about something and leaning in towards her. We couldn't hear what he was saying, but I didn't like it. What were we going to do?

There was an announcement about our train, and Mrs Reilly came over to us. She explained that the man was her husband and that she hadn't expected to see him there, and he would now be coming on the train with us to Phillip Island. That wasn't the way it was meant to be! We picked up our bags and boarded a small train with rows of seats either side of a long central aisle. I found myself facing Mrs Reilly and the man a distance from where they sat side by side at the head of the carriage. The train lurched and rattled through the night. We were tired and uneasy. The yellow lights of the carriage seemed to spotlight our lovely teacher and this horrible man who were still arguing and talking. All eventually became quiet. He had gone to sleep.

I have no memory whatsoever of where we got off or where we slept. Somehow, we reached the boys' home the next morning and met some boys. We saw Mrs Reilly's sons, who looked nice and had black curly hair. The building was big and bare inside, and we had to walk around outside in the cold quite a bit with these boys. I don't remember a thing about 'my' boy. I don't remember a thing about the trip back to Bendigo.

I felt that Mrs Reilly would get into trouble if the headmistress found out about the man coming with us, especially because he was drunk. For some reason, I felt a bit guilty. I didn't tell Mum.

It was a relief to be back in the classroom on Monday morning with Mrs Reilly doing the ordinary thing of marking the roll as usual. We girls didn't talk about our weekend, and it was good to get back to plain schoolwork.

I still liked Mrs Reilly a lot and would talk to her whenever I saw her in the playground. I decided that she must be lonely living at the school without her family and in a new country, so thought of asking if she would like to come with us to the drive-in cinema one Saturday night. Mum had met her at school, and although she liked her as well, she was a bit surprised by my idea. She needed persuading, but finally we organised an evening to see *The Purple Plain*, which I had looked up in *The Advertiser*. I knew it was a war book by H.E. Bates.

On the night, Mum and I drove into the back entrance of the school up the lane to the smaller single-storey boarding house where Mrs Reilly lived. Mum parked under the huge pepper tree while I ran in to knock on the door. I knew all about the layout because the boarding house was just near the tennis courts, and where Mr Sleeman parked his car. Mrs Reilly answered the door and off we went. She sat in the front and I, in the back seat.

It was getting dark as we drove along the street to join the end of the queue of cars lining up to turn left into the drive-in. At the ticket office, Mum leant out with the money for 'Two adults and one child,' and we were in. Mum and I knew how it all worked because our whole family loved going to the drive-in with the little kids in their pyjamas and a pile of blankets in the back seat. Mum drove along the rows till we found a spot pretty much in front of the centre of the big white screen. She parked on the little hill that was there to make us comfortable looking up at the screen. We hooked up the speaker to her window, wound the window up and turned it on. It was still just talking and advertisements.

I wanted to show Mrs Reilly the kiosk and café, which would be bright and full of food smells and people queuing to buy food, lollies, ice creams and drinks to take back to their cars. I didn't think she'd be interested in the playground beneath the screen, but she didn't want to go to the kiosk either. She and Mum stayed in the car talking while I ran to get some lollies. We all decided to sit on the bench front seat with me in the middle. It got darker and darker; the lights around the kiosk and the fence dimmed; the screen came alive and the speaker got louder, and the night started.

We had to get through the usual first half of film trailers and shorts but they didn't seem too long, and it was nice sitting there together watching them and talking about them a bit, which you could do at the drive-in as compared to the pictures. Then *The Purple Plain* started. It was very exciting and there were a couple of scary, startling bits, during one of which Mrs Reilly said, 'Ooh, hold my hand, Elizabeth. That'll feel better.' She took my hand and held it for the rest of the film in a friendly sort of way. I liked that but wondered if Mum thought it a bit odd. Holding hands wasn't something Mum did.

I enjoyed watching how the men survived in the desert and was interested to learn that sucking a pebble was a way to quench your thirst. We talked about that and other bits of the film as we drove Mrs Reilly back to school. I think she had a good time. She thanked us a lot when we dropped her off. The thanks were contagious, so as we drove home I too thanked Mum for taking us. I think she was a bit surprised.

Mrs Reilly taught us for just two years, and then, without any goodbyes, she wasn't there at the start of the next year. I would have liked to say goodbye. I hope that she found a good school to work in and was able to bring her boys home.

We had started learning science with a teacher who was lean, grey-haired and strict but who loved her subject, which made me love it too. In her first lesson, she brought in crystals which she had grown herself. The crystal I liked best was a copper sulphate one which was a brilliant clear blue, a couple of inches long, with clean, shiny facets. We started making some solutions to evaporate and crystallise in little glass dishes.

I decided to make a big crystal at home and went to the chemist in Eaglehawk to buy some copper sulphate. Making a big single crystal was harder than it seemed though, and I didn't have the patience or knowledge to isolate just one crystal and then encourage it to grow. I ended with a gloggy mass of tiny crystals and decided to just leave it all at that!

There was a lot of other good stuff to learn and do, like French. Learning a language was completely new to me, and by the end of our first few lessons, we were expected to be able to say the date of our birthday in French. *Fifteen* was *quinze*, which

I found quite hard to say the right way as it sounded so different from the way it looked. *Décembre* was easy. I never got my turn in class despite a lot of hand-waving, and that was a mixture of relief and disappointment. That pretty much sums up my French language experience. I could learn the words and the rules but was not at all good at pronouncing words or even hearing the words and sounds accurately. I'm still the same.

I really liked the way that a bell would ring to signal the end of each class. It was a real bell at the other end of the classrooms, and a monitor from one of the other levels was in charge of watching the time and leaving class to ring it. I'd pack away the books for that lesson into my desk and get out the ones for the next lesson. I had written out the timetable and stuck it on the inside of my desk lid because I liked knowing what was going to happen. So we'd be sitting there talking away, and in would walk the next teacher and off we'd go with something else.

Something new about senior school was that we had a visiting teacher for choir, which we did in the hall on Tuesday afternoons. I would sometimes get a bit giggly because she swayed around a lot and waved her arms and had a big trained voice with a lot of wobble in it. I knew that she was trained, just like Mr Masters was with his diving and his stylised walk on the board, but somehow I found it harder to take seriously. I was beginning to realise that I wasn't a very tuneful singer and that my voice actually didn't sound clear and strong like the girls who were good singers. I liked the songs though and enjoyed choir.

We were big girls now. One day the school gave us leaflets to take home advertising a mothers' and daughters' night at the School of Mines in Bendigo. So, one winter's night, Mum and I went out together to sit in the freezing hall with girls and their mothers from all the Bendigo schools. I already knew about periods and babies and what was called 'intercourse' but in a vague, detached sort of way and was interested to see what would happen. A lady got up on the stage and talked to us for a bit before introducing a black-and-white film which flickered up on the screen. There were diagrams of a uterus and fallopian tubes, some talk of menstruation and pads, maybe a diagram of a penis, not much new really. However, I liked the evening as it seemed special. We bought a booklet to take home.

Some things remained the same. We still went to the hall for PE with Mr Meredith but this time walked down the ramp and lined up at the door near the stage door and the bike shed. He now took us for sport too, in the big yard behind the junior school. We learnt softball in summer and netball in winter. I liked learning the new games and their rules, which were much more formal than the rules for rounders and dodgie. Our tennis teacher still came up from Melbourne every third Friday, and I would watch the time for my lesson and then slip out of class. I'd learn some tactics and then have some game practice with him and the other three girls in the lesson.

In senior school, we could book the tennis court to play at lunchtime, and there would be a fierce race on Monday morning to fill in a time on the tennis court blackboard and hope that the boarders hadn't got there first. It took a couple of years for me to get the courage to join in that race, and in the meantime, I could sit on the wall surrounding the court and watch the bigger girls play.

School was so good now that I hated having to miss a day because I might miss out. I might miss something fun, and the work was serious enough that I would have 'catching up' to do. I might miss something in French and then not know what the next lesson was about. Or I might miss starting a new bit of maths and not know how to do the problems.

Best of all, I felt that the teachers might actually like me.

This reinforced the resolve that I'd had from when I was about nine or ten that I needed an education. I did not want to be like my mother, having to do what my husband wanted, with no money of her own and looking after a house and children. The only women I knew who worked were shop assistants behind a counter, nurses, and teachers, who often seemed to be single and sometimes sour. In Eaglehawk, I knew that Miss Cook had been the chemist, but she was now retired and lived with her sister in a big house behind a high wooden fence bursting with blue plumbago. I never saw her. On the radio, the announcers were all men with English accents. The books I read had mothers who prepared picnics and whose role was that of a stay-at-home mother. I saw no professional women other than teachers. I wanted to get a proper education so that I could have a job that I was proud of and which would make me independent. This wasn't an urgent, anxious feeling but stood there as a foundation stone in the building of my life.

Chapter Sixteen
End Of Childhood

Form Two meant changing rooms and leaving my sky blue desk behind. We still had Mrs Reilly for English but now had to endure British history, which I thought was the most boring subject in the world – all those kings and queens! However, that was counter-balanced by South America in geography. It was such an interesting continent with a pleasing shape to draw, the long curvy range of the Andes and the magnificent Amazon River. I liked learning that the sea water was still fresh from the Amazon outflow for miles out from the coast. I still want to see the Amazon.

We not only changed rooms but the girls were changing. Over the summer holiday, a lot of them had grown breasts and bought bras to put them in. It was a bit surprising to see all that shapeliness in their school uniforms. At just twelve, I still only had little buds and was as flat-chested in my tunic as ever.

However, I now had a secret. On the bus coming home from the swimming club end of season picnic at Daylesford Lake, a boy and I had kissed. During that afternoon, the kids about my age, the juniors, had got sick of the lake and the picnic ground and gone up to the car park to sit in our bus. Because the big kids weren't there, we could go down to the back seats and hang about there. I got one corner of the back seat bench and one of my friends got the opposite one. It was a strange, exciting afternoon because he and I were talking and laughing with other and looking at each other so much that the other kids almost seemed not to be there.

When it was time to go home and everyone piled on to the bus, we got kicked out of the back seats, and I went and sat in one of the seats about two thirds down. The boy walked up the aisle and suddenly sat beside me. I was surprised and really happy. We drove off. It got darker and he put his arm around my shoulders. It felt nice and friendly so I leant in to him. Then he put his other arm around me and kissed me on the lips. It was lovely and I felt so nice and warm and happy. We kept on kissing and leaning our heads on each other's shoulders and hugging. In the middle of one kiss, I heard a little squeal and opened my eyes to see my girlfriend turned round from her seat in front of me, absolutely amazed. I'd never seen her eyes so wide. I closed mine again and kept on kissing until we got back to Bendigo. It was a happy end to summer.

Over these couple of years, I was growing upwards and the pencil marks on the door frame where we measured ourselves were moving up by inches. Quite suddenly, I was tall. I was standing round in the kitchen one afternoon talking to Mum when Dad came in and snapped, 'If you don't stand up straight, I'll have to put you in a back brace.' I was frightened and angry about that, especially as Dad himself had a curvy back, which it looked like I had inherited. I wasn't game to point that out though. At school, I was proud to move towards the top of the line at PE and be one of the tall girls.

The girls were squealier and gigglier and knew hit songs, which they sang in the classroom at recess time. Elvis Presley had appeared on the radio and one girl in our class would scream and pretend to faint if anyone said his name. I thought that was really stupid. Actually, I was a bit scared of Elvis and was relieved to find the much safer Pat Boone to like.

About that stage, when Pa wasn't living with us, I had moved from the 'girls' bedroom', where I'd always slept, down to the back bedroom by myself. The back room had been decorated for my brother with the idea that the three girls would sleep in the one room, and he would have a room to himself. However, he didn't like it, so we swapped. I liked sleeping in the bottom bunk and didn't mind being at the far end of the house. The only problem was that it was right next to the usually unlocked back door, and I would sometimes wake up and worry about that. I'd get up to check and turn the key, feeling relieved that I'd made myself safe.

Getting undressed one wintry night, I took off my panties and saw them streaked with dark red. It must be my first period. It had just jumped up and got me – out of nowhere!

'Mum!' I yelled. 'Mum!'

I stood there holding my panties.

'Mum!'

I finally heard her footsteps coming down the hall. She came into the room.

'Look!' I said, showing her the panties.

'Oh, Lizzie. Let me see. Yes, it's your period, darling.'

I stood there and burst into loud tears. She hugged me while I cried my heart out. I never cried but now I was devastated. Fuelling my black grief and shock was the knowledge that everything would be different now. I wasn't a free child any more but would have to be a girl teenager and then a woman. I felt hopeless and trapped.

Gradually, I stopped sobbing and stood there in my singlet and socks, hiccuping.

'I'll go and see if I've got a Modess.'

I knew that was what her sanitary napkins were called. I also knew she had to buy them at the chemist and always seemed embarrassed to have to do it. They would be very discreetly put in a paper bag behind the counter before being handed over. It was better if one of the women were serving and not the chemist himself.

'No, I haven't,' she said, reappearing. 'I'll just have to tear up a sheet and we'll safety-pin it to your singlet. My belt won't fit you.'

So I stood there while Mum folded up a little rectangle of torn up sheet and safety-pinned it to the front and back of my singlet. I got into my pyjamas, climbed into the cold bed and lay there feeling shocked, miserable and strange with those layers of cloth held between my legs. At least, she could find some safety pins even though they were my little sister's nappy-pins.

Next morning, I had to unpin myself to go to the toilet. The sheet pad didn't have much blood on it, and I had my shower while Mum went over the road to borrow some pads from Mary. I still didn't have the little elastic belt to hold the pad in place, so off I went in my nappy-pins. I didn't tell anyone. It wasn't much different physically, except for feeling tired, dull and uncomfortable with that stupid pad between my legs. Mum had wrapped up another one for me to change into at lunchtime. That meant I had to wait for the one toilet cubicle out of four with a bin in it and let the girls queuing behind me go into the others. It was so embarrassing.

I could see nothing good at all about these periods.

My childhood had gone – just like that!

Chapter Seventeen
Reflections

It must have been the hormones that turned me into a girl teenager. I became interested in clothes, boys and my appearance, none with particularly successful results! I continued to swim my summers away, enjoy school and do my homework with the quiet goal of going to university and getting the qualifications for a job that would make me independent. I had a rough idea that I would work till I was twenty-eight and then get married and have children.

Well, that didn't happen to plan! I completed my Arts Degree and Diploma of Education at Melbourne University and promptly got married, aged twenty-one and one month. I wasn't alone with this almost child-bride marriage as many of our friends from uni did the same. The pill was just appearing but was not easily available for unmarried women. I knew no unmarried couples who lived together. I was terrified of getting pregnant, and getting married at that age didn't seem as strange a thing to do as it does now.

I lost my way in this marriage. I didn't know how to live with another person and manage to satisfy both our needs while keeping my sense of self intact. My husband and I were fulfilling one of the models of a married couple which the society of the time offered: he, academically clever, devoted to his research, me the supportive wife. We had a child fairly soon and took on the traditional roles of father and mother. He was a strong, kind role model of a father, a better father than husband. I became a *Women's Weekly* wife.

The advice columns told me to support my husband by having the house tidy and calm for when he came home, having dinner ready to be just finished off and dished up, and the baby fed, bathed and ready to say goodnight to Daddy before being put to bed. I would work hard to have all the shopping, cleaning and food preparation done so we could have relaxing weekends together. But we never knew what to do with those weekends, and I realised that we didn't actually enjoy each other's company. We seemed to have little in common. I felt inadequate, unloved and not particularly liked.

Germaine Greer got me back on track. I read *The Female Eunuch* in a state of shock and exhilaration. She was writing about me! She gave me the language to think about my marriage and how I could maintain my integrity within it. The early 1970s were exciting times as the press was publishing articles about feminism and women's lives; these were women with whom I could identify.

It wasn't easy, but I was changing. The relationship wasn't. After seven years of marriage, I realised that I was too young to live unhappily for the rest of my life and, with sadness, left. Looking back, that was a risk worth taking, and I gradually reclaimed myself.

There is nothing like being a parent to make you reflect on your own childhood and on the way your parents raised you. I wanted my children to have the physical freedom which I'd had but also to feel a stronger sense of underlying security than I had experienced. The difficult task would be to find the ability to anticipate their needs and offer support and opportunities in a low-key way but not swamp them with expectations and advice. I wanted them to be 'known' by me and feel my support and generosity. Without then knowing the term, I wanted my children to have a 'free-range' childhood.

Living with my children in an urban environment was inevitably different from my childhood experience. My son was aged between two and five when we lived in a ground floor flat in London. The playgrounds were fenced or walled off from the surrounding roads. I supervised tricycle-riding up and down the footpath in front of our flat. I tried to be outside as much as possible and sat for hours watching him in the playground sandpit and spent more hours pushing swings. I tried to let him wander in these controlled environments, but there was nothing very interesting for him to do. I organised his friends to come and play. On return visits, I learnt that English children had huge amounts of indoor toys and played differently from Australian kids who were more used to being outside and playing physically.

Nine years later and in my second marriage, my husband Nick and I were living in North Fitzroy, a gentrifying inner suburb of Melbourne, in a terrace house with a backyard. We now had two daughters. From their babyhood, I asked Nick to take responsibility for the evening bath and story, and putting the girls to bed. I felt it was important for him to be part of the fabric of their lives and not just appear for the fun bits. He did this reliably and well and has said that, although it was difficult at times, he was very glad to have done it.

The children could go out the back door and play in the sandpit which we'd built for them or ride their trikes down the path to the back fence. Anything out the front door had to be supervised, just like London really. A couple of blocks away were Edinburgh Gardens, a traditional park with formal tree-lined paths to ride bikes on, a playground and a big black steam engine to climb over. It was good to go for a walk down there in the afternoon for an outing to the swings, but the space was too formal to offer anything intriguing to the children.

I was getting sick of finding a place to park the car in our increasingly crowded street, and in summer, having to seatbelt two small children into a furnace of a car. I was getting tired of walking slowly around hot asphalt streets holding one child's hand and pushing the other in her stroller. The view of next door's brick wall out of our side windows felt increasingly dismal.

I began looking back to my own childhood and forward to my children's future childhood. Somehow, my present, past and future lives and those of my children fused. I began to think about these young girls, one, eighteen months, and the other, a four-year-old, and to wonder what their lives would be like if we stayed put. I didn't know where they would be able to play and ride their bikes freely. I wanted them to be able to use their bodies and gain physical confidence. I didn't know where they would have privacy from my gaze and supervision. Our garden was too small. I didn't want to have to organise all their play, nor did I want them to go to schools with small asphalt playgrounds.

I needed to go somewhere where we all had space. I was sitting up in bed one Saturday morning reading the 'For Sale' ads in *The Age* newspaper when one ad jumped up from all the others. How could you have a house, bigger than ours, with a huge garden and the Yarra River just outside the bottom fence, for about the same amount of money our house could fetch? It seems you could in Warrandyte, a small township by the Yarra River, on the outskirts of the metropolitan area. This prospect was so exciting that we drove out that very afternoon.

The timber house was long and low, and its varnished pine cladding glowed in the winter sun. Huge gum trees rose above the grey roof. The driveway gate was open and we could see a big garage. The agent was showing someone else through the house and suggested we walk down the garden to have a look at the river out the bottom gate. We walked around the side of the house, past large rhododendrons, and faced the huge garden stretching down to the river. The grass extended to the bottom fence about fifty metres away. A tall white-trunked gum tree stood in the centre, towering above the liquidambars, camellias and the large poplars at the bottom. The air was fresh and fragrant. Down past the gum tree, we turned to look at the house and saw that it had a wide, recessed verandah overlooking the garden and the trees beyond. By now, I was weeping with recognition of the past and longing for the future. A small ramshackle wooden gate opened to the river reserve, and there, twenty metres in front of us, hidden by scrub and reached by a rough, eroded track, flowed the Yarra.

The river moved past us silently. It smelt cold, fresh and a bit muddy. On the opposite bank, trees grew thickly down to the water's edge and a bed of reeds caught the sun and quivered in the lighter current at the river's edge. All I could hear was a faint rustle of gum leaves and the insistent chiming of bellbirds. A kookaburra laughed in the distance. I think I had got used to background silence as a child, and here it was again.

I could not believe that a house with a river in front of it was within my reach. My childhood dreams spurred by Ratty and Mole and other books could be realised. Our children would be able to play and explore and have a physical freedom. My husband and I would have space and nature in our lives.

We bought the house and lived there for twenty-four years.

Over time, I realised that parts of Warrandyte were strangely like Eaglehawk. It too, had been a gold mining town, and the bush had the same sort of dry gravelly soil with smallish trees. I learnt that, like Eaglehawk, the soil had been completely churned over in the search for surface gold and that many sections of bush and trees here were regrowth. If you went off the walking tracks, there were the familiar occasional small pits in the ground. People still panned for gold in the reefs which rose to the surface of the river. This was a full-circle realisation.

The children played freely in our garden. They ran their billy cart about thirty or forty metres down the slope of the garden through the trees. This got a bit hair-raising to watch at times. We rigged up a high swing from one of the gum tree branches, and again it was best not to watch what happened on it.

They used to ride their bikes along the track outside our fence down to the swimming hole and beyond. They saw a platypus in the river. One day, our older daughter raced inside, white and excited. She'd ridden over a snake which had then entwined itself in her front wheel. She looked down and thought she had some bark tangled in her wheel. Then she saw it was a snake. She practically levitated off the bike and raced home with her friend. We all walked down to retrieve the bike but saw no sign of the snake. She wasn't put off and continued to ride around the bush paths.

I learnt to trust the children as I realised that they wouldn't tackle anything they couldn't do. Sometimes at a playground or somewhere, another mother would eye one of our daughters doing something a bit perilous and ask if I'd seen what was happening. I had, and would answer, 'Yes. She knows what she's doing.'

This free playing was encouraged by Warrandyte Primary School, whose policy on uniforms (in the mid-1980s) offered girls and boys the same uniform, with the option of a dress for girls. Our older daughter wore her uniform dress for one day only, her first day at school, when boys had sniggered at her while playing on the monkey bars. Rather than stop playing as she wished, from then on she wore pants!

The freedom gained by the relative physical isolation of our house was challenged by our dependence on the car. We needed it for shopping and taking and collecting from schools. Nick had a long trip to his work at Melbourne University and rather than financially struggle to buy another car, he bought a small motorbike and commuted on it for about sixteen years. He liked riding past the creeping cars at the city end of the freeway in Fitzroy.

It was becoming hard to manage on one income, and when both the washing machine and the fridge died within a couple of weeks of each other, it was too much and I went back to work, teaching at a nearby school. I was sorry to have to do that as our younger daughter was still a pre-schooler. Now I had to drive and collect the girls from before and after school care and family day care, joining the traffic jam at Warrandyte Bridge each morning as all the houses hidden in the bush spilled out their children, mothers and cars. There was far too much driving. By the time our younger daughter started school, an after-school programme organised by the school had started. Phew!

We were all freed up when the girls felt they were ready for the school bus which stopped at the top of our dirt road. They would walk the fifteen minutes up the road, in time for the bus, and the reverse would happen in the afternoon. I could usually get home from my school at pretty much the same time as they did. My husband sometimes worked at home and that helped a lot.

The confidence gained by catching the school bus spilled over into catching the local bus which stopped at the same place at the top of the road. When they were about nine, our younger daughter and her friend decided that they would be able to catch this bus over to Eastland, the local shopping centre, and back on a Saturday afternoon. Her friend's mum would drop him off at our place, and the two of them would set off up the hill to catch the bus. They'd worked out the bus timetable – important because it was a very infrequent service – and we had to trust them.

They would look very small as they headed off up the road. I never quite knew what they did at Eastland but was really impressed with the way they managed the system and how they always got themselves home roughly on time. Later, this adventure extended to catching the bus to Ringwood Station and then a train into the city. Again, they negotiated this perfectly well and would get home at the end of Saturday afternoon after a marathon day on public transport. I really admired their competence, but it was a bit nerve-racking thinking of these small children hitting the city streets on their own. This was well before mobile phones, but they knew how to use public phones and always had phone money with them.

I recently asked my daughters what they had been afraid of as children. One of them said, 'Only the things that adults made us do.'

'Like what?' I asked.

'Oh, going to school and after-school care.'

Clunk!

'Oh! I am sorry. You were very good at doing it anyway.'

'Well, I knew I had to, and I knew you had to go to work.'

I was sad about that but proud of her resilience. It was hard to get it right all the time.

This was in the 1980s, thirty years after my childhood. Germaine Greer and feminism had transformed the way I saw my role as a woman in society and in the family. I wanted my daughters to grow into a world where women had the same chances as men, and where people were treated equally. I tried to encourage our family to respect and be kind to each other and for the children to realise that we parents were people too and not superhuman or perfect.

About this time, I had taken a deep breath and asked Dad why he had belted me in my childhood. He was embarrassed. I think he said that he was sorry, but the apology got tangled up in an explanation that he thought his short temper must have been because his appendix had been playing up at the time. Well, that explained a little bit but did nothing much to help our relationship, which, from my mid-teens, had the quality of a truce. I always had an underlying wariness of his sarcastic tongue.

As I got older and less bouncy, and he became calmer, we had been able to have some common ground in what I was learning at school, what I was reading and our shared enjoyment of the quirks of language. He had an endearing quality of walking out of the room and returning with a book or newspaper cutting to illustrate or enhance something we were talking about. I laugh at myself these days, as I reach for my phone and go to Google in the middle of a discussion. I wonder if Dad would have loved or hated Google.

His life was quiet and self-absorbed as he moved between his work, music, gardening and reading. There was a lot to admire about Dad, and I value what he gave me in providing an environment of books, reading and love of language.

Reading and books were important to me as we raised our children. Because *Scuffy the Tugboat* and *Tootle* had been my favourite Golden Books in my early childhood in the late 1940s, now, in the late seventies and early eighties, I looked forward to sharing them with my children. However, as I read both out loud to my daughters, I was startled to have a very clear personal reaction to the way that Tootle's urge for freedom to play was controlled by the men with red flags stopping him doing just that. Similarly, Scuffy was brought home from his adventure to merely sail in the bath. I didn't want my young, lively, playful children to be imbibing such a controlling 1950s view of the world, where conformity and work were modelled and praised. I had felt sorry for the train and tugboat as a child but didn't realise they were being praised for conformity. These two books really alerted me to the messages our children receive from their stories.

First, I was conscious of having girl children and how important it was for me to provide them with as little gender stereotyping as possible. I became pretty adept at doing some editorialising during and after a story. 'Look how high she jumped! ... She was really clever getting out of that situation, wasn't she! ... Goodness! Why did she do that?' and so on.

I would use 'she' instead of the universal 'he' so that they would feel their gender was an equal part of the world. And similarly, I would try to choose books, like *The Practical Princess*, that gave girls an active role. If a female expert came on during the TV news, I had to restrain myself from saying, 'Look! It's a woman!' I wanted the girls to think that this was normal, not even worth getting excited over. The reaction was more mine. It was so different from my childhood experience of women.

The second message from Tootle and Scuffy exemplifies a big issue confronting a parent and a child. What is the balance between freedom and restraint? How much can your child be trusted to keep herself safe if left to play in the metaphorical meadow or stream? What are the safeguards that you can put in place and what safeguards exist in your child's community? Where does the parental responsibility for the child's physical wellbeing, her social and emotional development and the development of her skills and interests begin and end?

From the child's viewpoint, how does a child learn to be free and safe and trusted? She cannot do everything for herself and needs interest and insight from her parents to help support her as she grows up. She needs to be trusted.

For me, wide reading provided part of the answer. I found that reading gave me a sense of freedom but also suggested ways of controlling risk. Books can also introduce ethical dilemmas and ways of behaving responsibly.

I've also been thinking about free-range grand-parenting. Looking at how my children raise their children has made me wonder what part of their own childhood they choose to include in their roles as parents. I remember Mum's love and acceptance of me as a child. I realise now that she understood my need to be free, and I respect that she didn't fight my urge to play as I wished. Sometimes, I'd have liked to be pulled in a bit and be offered some choices or guidance in life. However, that was not the way she was. I notice how my children's personalities affect their parenting, how their methods blend with those of their partners and how the combination works. I remember the constant choices and decisions a parent has to make.

It's a sort of re-mothering where I bring what I have learnt in life to my grandchildren. It's a different but repeated experience and a relief to do it at a 'hands-off' distance from the intensity of actual parenting. I am aware that I don't know these new grandchildren as well as I knew my own children; therefore, it is a bit harder to judge what they can and cannot do, or how they might react to something I do or say. This means I must take a step back until I feel I know the situation. The responsibility is very different.

Just like a parent, I want to document precious moments with a grandchild, and it's so easy with a phone camera. I've sat in front of a grandchild, holding the phone between my eyes and theirs and taken photos – for later. I realised that I was looking at the child through a lens. The child not seeing the gaze of her grandmother but the gaze of the lens. And I was not part of that 'spontaneous' moment but had turned it into documentation or performance.

However, if I think back to when I was a child, there would

have been times when I'd have liked the immediacy of the image that a phone camera gives. It's such a far cry from the black box camera with its little shiny window that you had to move around to focus properly before you took the photo.

I realised that there are active and passive photographs. A passive photo would have the child directed and made to pose by the photographer. An active photo would be one where the child has power over the image that is being taken of her and arranges herself how she wants to be seen.

Being photographed frequently can invade a child's sense of privacy. I feel that the spontaneity and freedom of the moment is altered and the photographed children are alerted to the fact that they are being watched. The personal nature of the play or experience has been taken from them and often shared with the world. I love to receive the photos of my grandchildren on Instagram or email. It's all so immediate. No waiting for the film to be developed. But I wonder if the presence of adults standing around with cameras inhibits the play or encourages performance and posturing. I don't like the way that, from a very early age, little girls learn from their screens how to pose in a stylised and sexy manner.

However, there could be a kids' backlash. I've seen older children wearing T-shirts saying 'No Photos' and Instagrams of younger kids poking out their tongues at the camera and looking grumpy.

I'm interested in the media discussion of contemporary child-rearing practices, where I find terms such as 'helicopter parents', 'dragon mothers', 'perfectionist parents' and 'free-range children'. I note that the name of the first three styles refers to the behaviour of the parents and the latter to the needs of the child.

Some balanced academic discussion can be found amongst the mass of information on the internet, most of which focuses heavily on the American 'free-range children' movement led by Lenore Skenazy. But more common are pictures of road signs warning of 'Free-Range Children' and advertisements for childcare centres describing themselves as 'free-range'. There are heated discussions about the right to leave sleeping babies in cars and demands to support the couple who were prosecuted for allowing their children to walk to school. 'Free-range' is often associated with neglect. An article claims that 'we don't need that sort of thing here in Australia'.

I see countless pictures of allegedly 'free-range' children posing in picturesque settings. Well, to me, these are just photos of kids having a good time on a family outing. The parents are very clearly present and supervising. The child is again the object of the parental focus. I'm suspicious of some concepts of 'free-range' children because it seems that type of parenting is not so very different from some of the more controlled 'free-range' chicken farming.

The City of Bendigo, through the work of the council and its supporters, has been designated the first Australian UNICEF Child Friendly City. There are plans to make walking paths safe for 'free-range children'. A 'free-ranging walk' was launched in 2012 by Lenore Skenazy. It is a planned route with a map, points to look at and suggestions about the time needed to walk each stage.

Bendigo's initiative is good. It addresses the issue that towns are now generally perceived as being dangerous for children. The resulting constriction, by parents, of free and independent movement of their children deprives children of their chance to grow into the wider community. This statement by community environmentalist David Engwicht captures precisely what I experienced as a child and what now seems to be lost:

'Changing streets from places to "movement corridors" robs children of the opportunity to explore their neighbourhood in ever increasing circles as they mature. This freedom to explore the local neighbourhood is probably the key ingredient in children feeling they belong to a neighbourhood, a place. It not only gives them the opportunity to develop relationships with people of all ages who live in their neighbourhood, it gives them the opportunity to develop a relationship with the *placeness* of their physical environment. Robbing children of a sense of place is robbing them of the very essence of life.' (*Towards an Eco-City: Calming the Traffic*)

I was allowed to roam freely and develop a love of and connection with my small town and its people. I learned to make choices, take risks and, in doing so, find my own limits. Having learned in childhood to be physically and mentally brave gave me the confidence in adult life to trust that my children could do the same.

I think that for most of the time, the parents of an authentically free-range child do not impose an intense adult gaze on their child. Their challenge is to walk the tightrope between control and neglect whilst balancing the complex relationship of parent and child. If that is achieved, the child is then safe within her freedom as she learns to navigate, negotiate and take responsibility for her life.

Epilogue

Saturday, March 18, 2017.

Richard rang at 3.30 pm, and I knew by the silence that Mum had finally died. When he could speak, he told me that she had only just died, her breaths fading away within the two minutes since he had said, 'Goodbye, Mum.'

I was engulfed by a wave of diffuse emotion. Mum was ninety-five, and her thin, little body had been deteriorating for years and years. She had endured her last illness, pneumonia, for about a week, and we had all had time to sit with her and say goodbye.

Nick and I were at the beach house, having a rest from the nursing home visits, while Rich was spending time with Mum. I wandered around the house looking out at the sun and trees, not knowing what to do with what was going on in my head. I decided I needed a swim.

I wanted to purify our relationship and wash away the memories of the last years: the duty, the endless driving to visit the nursing home, the decisions and the constant feeling that there was something more I could do to make her comfortable. I had felt horror on feeling her tiny birdlike back within my hugs. I didn't want to remember those things. I wanted to wash her clean and bright.

It was a hot afternoon. We made the ritual walk through

the tea tree path, over the trunk of the reclining tea tree, over the little dune to see bubby beach at low tide. A reef platform reaches into the ocean and protects the little bay. It is a beach for all ages and sizes.

I walked past babies, children, teenagers, parents and grandparents. Past the tanned and the pale-skinned, the skinny and the obese, the smooth young skin and the skin falling in folds over old bodies.

My mother had died one hour and fifteen minutes ago, and I walked with this knowledge within my very being. I was an isolated pillar of emotion.

I walked out to sea, and as the warm water of low tide rose past my knees, thighs, hips and waist, I remembered Mum laughing and telling me how much she had loved swimming at the Sydney beaches of her childhood.

I pushed off, ducked under to be totally immersed and swam a few strokes out before flipping on to my back and backstroking out on the safe, supporting sea. Looking back to shore, I saw the pines, tea tree and little dunes curving around the faded green life-saving clubhouse, all fringed by golden sand.

I left the other bathers behind and quietly trod water as I faced the indigo horizon. My eyes were level with the dark blue out there. I floated, relishing the support and the gentle pressure of the deep, pure green-blue water. Lacy frills of surf broke on the far reef. I lay suspended and quiet within the sea's embrace. I was a baby, lying on the bosom of my mother, feeling her quiet breathing and warm enclosing arms.

Tendrils of cooler water slipped past my body. Small waves raised and lowered me as the tide began to turn. It was time to swim ashore to the open, uncharted territory of an entirely new phase of my life.

Acknowledgements

I owe gratitude in both the personal and professional spheres. Personally, I would like to thank my husband, Nick Low, for his listening, reading and discussion as I brought what was initially a patchwork of stories into a coherent piece of writing. His encouragement was unwavering, as was his patience with me and the vagaries of my interaction with the laptop.

Richard and Sally Trembath, my brother and sister, offered support. Richard read the manuscript carefully and made valuable, detailed comments. My other sister, Jane, died in 2005, and I am sad that she can't share this experience with us.

Input from my children, Andrew, Vinca and Jenny, was always encouraging and helpful.

Nick, Dorothy Bennett and I had formed a small writing group to read and discuss each other's offerings. Dorothy encouraged me to publish my stories.

I returned to Eaglehawk and Bendigo to check some of my memories. Eaglehawk Heritage Society and the Goldfield Libraries were generous with their time and help. My school, Girton, now much expanded and a very different place from my childhood, welcomed me warmly.

Professionally, I'd like to acknowledge the work of Dr Carolyn Whitzman (at the University of Melbourne) and Dr Julie Rudner (at La Trobe University) on the importance of childhood independent mobility, the need for children to experience risk-taking behaviour within their capacity to manage risks, and the child's need to grow in a local environment which encourages safe exploration.

Writers Victoria offered a range of support. Josiane Behmoiras assessed my manuscript and made important suggestions regarding structure. She gave me the confidence to insert my adult self into the narrative. A Writers Victoria 'pitching' workshop run by Melanie Ostell gave me a hard dose of the reality of getting published.

Brolga Publishing made that aspiration a reality. Mark Zocchi led me through the process of developing the manuscript into the finished book. Alice Cannet read and understood my work and then edited it sympathetically and thoughtfully. Elly Cridland, the typesetter, helped with font choices. I enjoyed the co-operative process of publishing with Brolga.

Finally, I thank Eaglehawk. It was a place where I could spread my childhood wings.

Eaglehawk Girl
Liz Low

ISBN: 9780648327721   Qty

RRP   AU$24.99   .....

Postage within Australia   AU$5.00   .....

TOTAL* $_____

* All prices include GST

Name: ....

Address: ....

....

Phone: ....

Email: ....

Payment: [ ] Money Order   [ ] Cheque   [ ] MasterCard   [ ] Visa

Cardholder's Name: ....

Credit Card Number: ....

Signature: ....

Expiry Date: ....

Allow 7 days for delivery.

Payment to: Marzocco Consultancy (ABN 14 067 257 390)
                   PO Box 12544
                   A'Beckett Street, Melbourne, 8006
                   Victoria, Australia
                   admin@brolgapublishing.com.au

BE PUBLISHED

Publish through a successful publisher.
Brolga Publishing is represented through:
• National book trade distribution, including sales,
marketing & distribution through Woodslane Pty Ltd
• International book trade distribution to:
    - The United Kingdom
    - North America
    - Sales representation in South East Asia
• Worldwide e-Book distribution

For details and enquiries, contact:
Brolga Publishing Pty Ltd
PO Box 12544
A'Beckett St
Melbourne, Vic 8006
markzocchi@brolgapublishing.com.au
(Email for a catalogue request)

www.ingramcontent.com/pod-product-compliance
Lightning Source LLC
Chambersburg PA
CBHW062207270326
41930CB00009B/1673